Shakespeare and Political Theat

Shakespeare in Practice

Series Editors:

Stuart Hampton-Reeves, Professor of Research-informed Teaching, University of Central Lancashire, UK, and Head of the British Shakespeare Association

Bridget Escolme, Reader in Drama, Queen Mary, University of London, UK

Published:

Stephen Purcell
SHAKESPEARE AND AUDIENCE IN PRACTICE

Andrew James Hartley
SHAKESPEARE AND POLITICAL THEATRE IN PRACTICE

Forthcoming:

Don Weingust
SHAKESPEARE AND ORIGINAL PRACTICES

Darren Tunstall
SHAKESPEARE AND GESTURE IN PRACTICE

Bridget Escolme
SHAKESPEARE AND SITE-SPECIFIC PERFORMANCE IN PRACTICE

Kathryn Prince
SHAKESPEARE AND SPACE IN PRACTICE

Paul Prescott
SHAKESPEARE AND REVIEWING PERFORMANCE IN PRACTICE

Alexander Huang
SHAKESPEARE AND DIASPORA IN PRACTICE

Kevin Ewert
SHAKESPEARE AND DIRECTING IN PRACTICE

**Shakespeare in Practice
Series standing order
ISBN 978–0–230–27637–6 hardcover
ISBN 978–0–230–27638–3 paperback**
(*outside North America only*)

You can receive future titles in this series as they are published by placing a standing order. Please contact your bookseller or, in case of difficulty, write to us at the address below with your name and address, the title of the series and the ISBN quoted above.

Customer Services Department, Macmillan Distribution Ltd, Houndmills, Basingstoke, Hampshire RG21 6XS, England

Shakespeare and Political Theatre in Practice

Andrew James Hartley

© Andrew James Hartley 2013

All rights reserved. No reproduction, copy or transmission of this publication may be made without written permission.

No portion of this publication may be reproduced, copied or transmitted save with written permission or in accordance with the provisions of the Copyright, Designs and Patents Act 1988, or under the terms of any licence permitting limited copying issued by the Copyright Licensing Agency, Saffron House, 6–10 Kirby Street, London EC1N 8TS.

Any person who does any unauthorized act in relation to this publication may be liable to criminal prosecution and civil claims for damages.

The author has asserted his right to be identified as the author of this work in accordance with the Copyright, Designs and Patents Act 1988.

First published 2013 by
PALGRAVE MACMILLAN

Palgrave Macmillan in the UK is an imprint of Macmillan Publishers Limited, registered in England, company number 785998, of Houndmills, Basingstoke, Hampshire RG21 6XS.

Palgrave Macmillan in the US is a division of St Martin's Press LLC, 175 Fifth Avenue, New York, NY 10010.

Palgrave Macmillan is the global academic imprint of the above companies and has companies and representatives throughout the world.

Palgrave® and Macmillan® are registered trademarks in the United States, the United Kingdom, Europe and other countries.

ISBN 978–0–230–37006–7 hardback
ISBN 978–0–230–37007–4 paperback

This book is printed on paper suitable for recycling and made from fully managed and sustained forest sources. Logging, pulping and manufacturing processes are expected to conform to the environmental regulations of the country of origin.

A catalogue record for this book is available from the British Library.

A catalog record for this book is available from the Library of Congress.

Printed in China

Contents

Acknowledgements vi
Series Editors' Preface vii

Introduction 1

Part I In Theory 9
1 The Politics of the Stage 11
2 The Curious Case of Mr Shakespeare 34

Part II In Practice 57
3 Identity Politics and the Stage 59
4 "Who talks of my nation?" Challenging the Establishment 75
5 "Let him be Caesar": Representing Politics 90
6 Place and Pedagogy: Site-Specific Production, School Tours, Prison Shakespeare, and the Question of Agenda 103
7 The Tame Snake: The Politics of Safe Shakespeare 116

Part III Provocation and Debate 129
8 "A Conversation with Ayanna Thompson in Three Acts" 131

Part IV Annotated Reading List 149

Notes 157
Bibliography 162
Index 166

Acknowledgements

I would like to thank Stuart Hampton-Reeves and Bridget Escolme for inviting me to propose this book and for their editorial care and attention thereafter. Thanks also to Cassie Cheney for helping in preparation of the final manuscript; to my friends and colleagues at UNC Charlotte, particularly Kirk Melnikoff, Mark Pizzato, James Vesce, and Jeanmarie Higgins; and to my family for their patience and support.

Series Editors' Preface

The books in the *Shakespeare in Practice* series chart new directions for a performance approach to Shakespeare. They represent the diverse and exciting work being undertaken by a new generation of Shakespeareans who have either come to the field from practice or have developed a career that combines academic work with theatrical practice. Many of these authors are based in Drama departments and use practical workshops for both teaching and research. They are conversant with the fields of English Literature and Performance Studies, and they move freely between them. This series gives them an opportunity to explore the hinterland between both and to give a greater prominence to some of the key questions that occupy performance studies in the study of Shakespeare.

We intend this series to shape the way in which Shakespeare in performance is taught and researched. Our authors approach performance as a creative practice, which can be treated as a work of art in its own right. We want to create a new curriculum for Shakespeare in performance, which embraces the full complexity of the art of theatre and is underpinned by performance theory.

The first part of each book explores the theoretical issues at stake, often drawing on key works in performance studies as well as seminal writings by theatre practitioners. The second part of the book consists of a series of critical studies of performance in practice, drawing on theatre history but chiefly focusing on contemporary productions and practitioners. Finally, we have asked all of our authors to engage in a debate with another scholar or practitioner so that each book ends on a note of provisionality and unresolved debate.

All of our books draw on a wide range of plays so that teachers can choose which plays they want to focus on. There will be no volume on *Hamlet, A Midsummer Night's Dream* or *Romeo and Juliet* – every volume can be used as a model for every play in the canon. Similarly, none of the books exhaust the research possibilities that they open: there is more, much more, work to be done on every topic in this series.

Studies of Shakespeare in performance often leave aside the audience. Either the critic's own response is used to voice the audience, or the audience is effaced altogether. Questions about the role of the audience in constructing the theatrical event are often posed, but rarely answered, at conferences and seminars. Leaving the audience out of theatrical analysis is problematic, but including them is, if anything, even more problematic. How does one give voice to an audience? Is an audience exterior to the performance, or is it part of it – in which case, it is possible to 'read' the audience in a critical way? What research tools do we need to conduct such work? Or is the audience an illusion? Stephen Purcell's addresses how notions of audience, audience configuration, audience expectation and audiences as they figure in play texts all produce meaning in the theatre. His work is the ideal book with which to begin this series.

The development of political theatre in the twentieth century has had a profound influence on the performance of Shakespeare's work. In a sense, Shakespeare's theatre has always been a political one which is keenly aware of its context. His earliest plays vividly dramatize the power games at the heart of England's bloody civil wars in the fifteenth century, and throughout his career, Shakespeare returned again and again to critical questions of authority, identity and transgression. This is one of the reasons why Bertolt Brecht studied the Elizabethan theatre, among other forms, when developing the "alienation" effect for his own highly politicized theatre. One of the consequences of Brecht's work, together with many other innovators from the last century, is that we can no longer approach Shakespeare performance in a neutral way. Andrew James Hartley's study is an important contribution to the series which demonstrates the potency (and the danger) of politicizing Shakespeare in performance.

Stuart Hampton-Reeves
Bridget Escolme

Introduction

In the summer of 2001, I was working as a dramaturg on a Georgia Shakespeare production of *Julius Caesar* which was set in the American south of the 1930s. One of the play's most disturbing scenes takes place right after Mark Antony has inflamed the crowd during his funeral oration over Caesar's corpse. Subtly manipulating the people's sympathies and loyalties, Antony is able to take an assembly of ordinary citizens, invert their leanings entirely, and turn them into a ravening and murderous mob. Once unleashed, they tear through the streets of Rome looking for anyone who might have been connected to the conspirators who assassinated Caesar. When they happen on a man who shares a name—Cinna—with one of the conspirators, they assault and kill him, knowing full well that he is merely a hapless poet who has nothing to do with the corpse Antony showed them in the forum. It's a chilling study in mob violence run amok, a moment so unsettling that it was consistently cut from all eighteenth- and nineteenth-century productions.

It is also part of a remarkably sustained study of the politics of manipulation, an idea which dominates *Julius Caesar* as a whole and the crowd scenes in particular. During the funeral oration which generates the arbitrary violence which follows it, Antony is a performer using words, gestures, and props (the bloody mantle around Caesar's body, for instance) to steer his audience into outrage and insurrection. In its "set-piece" nature, the funeral oration plays to both the onstage audience (the Roman crowd) and the offstage audience, those sitting in the actual theatre auditorium, probably in the dark, watching and listening. Antony's speech thus has multiple political consequences because the audience in the house is both being swayed by the oration and watching its effect on another audience contained within the fiction of the play. In this, it is not simply the logic of Antony's argument, but the way the character as personated by the actor uses his lines (and presence and gesture etc.) to best effect, which determines the political reach of the moment. The actor's choices—and therefore those of the director and the company in general—shape the speech, and those less conscious or deliberate theatrical effects (which might include his stumbling over his lines or doing other things which are not truly intentional) shape the political resonance of the moment in ways not determined by the text alone. Is he reasoned, or passionate, slow and reflective, or rushed and impulsive? Is he clearly distraught over the death of his friend, or is he measured and deliberate? Is he static or mobile, haughty or approachable? Does he seem driven by grief, the impulse to revenge or other concerns entirely, and does the production endorse those apparent feelings or suggest that they are being faked for the crowd's benefit? How does his physical placement on stage, the lighting and architecture of the set or the theatre itself bolster the overall effect on the audience? These concerns are not determined by the words on the page, so much of the moment's theatrical effect is determined by the immediate conditions of the production rather than by the play as written.

The forum scene is both politics at its most theatrical and theatre at its most political, not simply because it represents politics on stage but because it has—or can have—political effects on the offstage audience. As the scene progresses and transitions into the next, it becomes a nice marker of how performative debate can turn into propaganda and audience hysteria. Yet, whatever Antony's goals in the forum scene were, the death of Cinna the poet was fairly certainly not one of them, and the horror of the subsequent scene stems from its representation of Cinna's death as arbitrary or—to use one of the phrases we hear a lot in reports of military action—collateral damage. This is not an idea contrary to the idea of theatre as a political tool, though it does complicate that idea, reminding us that however much we (after Stanislavski) have come to privilege "motivation" in the generation of theatrical meaning (in what an actor intends to portray, for instance) theatrical semiotics—the way the production generates meaning—are notoriously erratic and hard to control. Audiences "misread" the action on stage, or they are affected by prior assumptions which they bring to the production. They get distracted or bored in ways which alter their sense of what they are seeing or hearing and they are—most importantly—plural. Audiences do not respond in unison, and what makes one audience member weep might make another, watching the same show, laugh.

In that 2001 production in Atlanta, the murder of Cinna the poet was staged as an Old South lynching, a white mob seizing a young black man and hanging him on stage. It was a bold and incendiary gesture designed by the director (John Dillon) to tap into his audience's memories of times not so very long ago, of making the production of an old play representing still older political realities immediate and provocative.

And, in a sense, it worked, but not as we had expected.

Two weeks before the production opened, terrorists commandeered three passenger jets and crashed them into the Pentagon and the twin towers in New York. The effects on the national psyche were immediate and all-consuming. In the days after the attacks, there was also a spate of reprisal assaults on Arab Americans. According to numerous overheard lobby conversations and audience talk back sessions, it was these reprisal attacks which the audience saw in the murder of Cinna the poet more than the civil rights era lynchings which the production had targeted. What that *meant* for each audience member in political terms, I cannot begin to guess, beyond speculating that the show seemed to be weighing in on the then common xenophobic debate about whether all Moslems or Arabs were potential terrorists. What was clear was that the action had become suddenly and unexpectedly immediate, tapping into a very specific aspect of the cultural zeitgeist and accruing weight and meaning we could not possibly have anticipated. The carefully constructed semiotics of the theatrical moment as we had envisaged it, were overwritten by what the audience brought with them into the auditorium, and the production's meaning changed. This fundamental instability is at the very heart of what theatre is, and it is part of what makes theatrical performance potent as a political tool but so erratic in its effects that they become difficult to track and assess.

In the most general sense, all theatre is political since it partakes of the same reality as the rest of life and is therefore bound to issues of power, economics and the competing social forces which frame selfhood and community. Critics like Benjamin Bennett go so far as to suggest that all theatre is inherently subversive because the experience of being in the audience of live theatre resists the hermeneutics of the literary, so that performance (rather than text or the theatre as institution) is innately revolutionary. The present study concentrates, however, on theatre which is expressly political in its focus, though the nature and scale of that focus vary significantly. Some of the productions in question are aggressively radical, challenging the fundamental assumptions of the social order; others channel their political energies more finely, targeting perhaps only a single issue for a few short moments of stage time during an otherwise seemingly apolitical production.

This book provides a source study of ideas, debates, and examples tied to the political dimensions of an expressly theatrical Shakespeare, serving, I hope, as a guide to students, teachers, and theatre practitioners. Its purpose is to explore Shakespeare in political terms which go beyond the consideration of the plays as text, instead focusing on performance practice in theoretical and material terms which attempt to unpack the nature, agenda, limits and potential of staged Shakespeare. It does so by contextualizing the specifics of particular plays not in terms of Early modern history but through a consideration of how the political valences of the plays in performance are shaped by non-literary concerns such as casting, venue, aesthetics, marketing, and audience demographics.

The shelves of university libraries are crammed with books enacting political readings of Shakespeare's plays. There is also a substantial body of theory and criticism on the theatre as an expressly political or politicized realm, and studies of individual plays in performance often wrestle with the political conditions surrounding a particular staging. This study, by contrast, approaches the politics of Shakespeare in performance in terms of the issues themselves, drawing on a selection of representative plays for specific instances. In the process, it aims to bridge the seeming fissure between an increasingly politicized approach to Shakespeare's text (particularly in the university classroom) and a theatrical culture which sometimes seems resistant to what are assumed to be the flattening schematics of political readings.

The book is divided into three distinct parts: an overall theoretical consideration of the issues, a series of chapters on specific instances as manifested in production and a dialogue about the book's contents with critic Ayanna Thompson. It concludes with an annotated reading list for those who wish to consider the subject further or in greater depth.

Chapter 1 provides an overview of some of the key issues in the consideration of theatrical politics, foregrounding the semantics and semiotics of space/venue, actor–audience dynamic and other non-literary components of performance. These concerns are framed by those authors most invested in an expressly political concept of theatre. I begin with a consideration of the epic theatre of Brecht and Piscator, their interest in exposing the socio-economic mechanisms behind character, their appeal to reason as well as to emotion and aesthetics and their interest in representing general causality over individual accident. My focus is on their work as theorists and theatre practitioners engaged in the material specifics of performance, rather than on their work as playwrights, giving special consideration to such resilient concepts such as *Verfremdungseffekte* or the "alienation effect." I touch on Zygmunt Hubner's notion of "theatre that fights" and on Ric Knowles' view of theatre as a crucially material and local phenomenon in the assessment of its political dimension. I move on to consider Augusto Boal's theatre of the oppressed and tie it to the broader notion of radical performance in contemporary culture presented by Baz Kershaw, leading to the following questions: can contemporary theatre ever escape containment by the so-called *establishment*, and if so, should its goals be intellectual, emotional or material? What is the relationship between dramatic political content and theatrical venue, and how do we assess political impact in terms not of company intent or the content of the script but audience response, which is—finally—where theatrical meaning resides?

If some forms of theatre are bound to commodity fetishism and ideological uniformity, what of Shakespeare which is so thoroughly embedded in Western culture's structures of power and elitism? This is the driving question behind Chapter 2 "The Curious Case of Mr. Shakespeare." Can theatrical Shakespeare ever be subversive or does his status always make him part of the establishment? Cultural materialism and new historicism have found ways to make political readings of text, especially in terms of gender, race and class, but in performance, identity politics is subsumed within larger framing ideological narratives and circumstances, many of them bound to economics. Is it the aegis of respectability, the distancing archaism of plot, character, and utterance or (paradoxically) their very familiarity which hamstring the plays' political dimension, and if so, what strategies might companies use to facilitate more politically incisive productions? Is the so-called democratizing impulse to bring Shakespeare to less privileged groups mere proselytizing, a necessarily subordination to elitist hegemony, or can it be meaningfully empowering? How do political productions circumvent the charge of being somehow "unShakespearean," or subvert the delegitimizing logic inherent in such a charge?

Part II, "In Practice," begins with a chapter on identity politics and the stage, focusing on *The Taming of the Shrew, Othello,* and *The Merchant of Venice* (Chapter 3). Each has a vexed history which hinges, in part, on casting. How are the politics of these plays different in performance than they are as literary texts, and how has their place in the material world of practical theatre been inflected politically? Does theatre necessarily subordinate the larger political concerns inherent in such issues to notions of character, and how does the presentism inherent in theatrical experience mitigate against a historical understanding of the original political conditions which inform the play? Is staged Shakespeare doomed to fight political battles which have been long concluded, or might they retain a contemporary edge albeit of a different kind from that felt by his original audience? I consider the way recent history has affected the construction of political meaning around recent stage productions of the three plays listed particularly in terms of casting and "cross"-casting for race and gender (the all-female *The Taming of the Shrew* at the Globe in 2003, Patrick Stewart's "photo negative" *Othello* at a theatre in Washington DC in 1997 and Peter Sellars's multiracial *The Merchant of Venice* at the Goodman in 1994).

Chapter 4 considers overtly anti-establishment productions of Shakespeare, making particular use of Michael Bogdanov's English Shakespeare Company productions of *Henry IV* and *V* (and their locational failures on tour) and a cluster of *Macbeth* productions from the 2000s, which attempted to navigate the contemporary political climate, particularly the US-led wars in Iraq and Afghanistan.

Chapter 5 focuses on *Julius Caesar*, particularly the representation of the Roman populace and crowd scenes on stage, tracking the way different productions have approached these notoriously difficult moments in terms of an attitude to the intelligence, agency, and manipulation of the public. The chapter considers recent Royal Shakespeare Company offerings in the light of current events and explores non-anglophone productions (German, Dutch and South African [Falk Richter, 2007; Van Hove, 2009; Yael Farber, 2001]) which have represented the funeral orations as studies in media "spin."

I move on to consider how non-traditional performance spaces inflect the work of a production and the audience's sense of what Shakespeare is, using examples from found space and promenade productions to consider how the politics of a play might be mapped onto the immediate locale and, by extension, its resident community (Chapter 6). The chapter then moves to consider school tours and prison productions as politically weighted subsets of the site-specific production model, exploring how they function in negotiating the cultural divide they inevitably inhabit and to what end.

Chapter 7 fastens on a particular university production to investigate how companies negotiate charges of inauthenticity while finding ways to make staged Shakespeare compelling, interesting, even subversive from "inside" the expectations of mainstream audiences and—particularly—educators. My consideration of UNC Charlotte's staging of *A Midsummer Night's Dream* extends the logic of the site-specific production model in its analysis of how a play generally considered "safe" for all audiences (including school children) might be made provocatively topical without simply alienating those who came to see it.

Chapter 8 (Part III) is a dialogue between the author and Ayanna Thompson, best known for her work on Shakespeare and race, particularly on African American performance. In this concluding exchange, we discuss what constitutes political theatre (including productions which lean to the right as well as to the left), how political productions might navigate the threat of audience disapproval in a climate where such disapproval could jeopardize the company's financial security, and the way that the goals of political productions vary from show to show, even from moment to moment, in ways which shift a sense of whether the value is in the making or the reception of the production.

Part I
In Theory

1
The Politics of the Stage

Assessing the political nature and impact of theatre is a complex business, in part because the nature of the theatrical event is difficult to limit and measure and because it is so ephemeral. Theatre, unlike a literary text, happens in a particular time and space, after which it becomes something else entirely, something potentially still potent, but generically different. Its meanings are shaped as much by light and music and the appearance of the actors as they are by the details of the dramatic script which is performed. As a result, theatre is an essentially experiential art form, and the meanings it generates—including its political meanings—tend to be limited to those who make up its audience. After it closes, the production may live on in memory, in reviews, in archive photographs or video, but it loses its kinetic immediacy, its presentness. It becomes disconnected from that which defined it: a crucially interactive dependence on the live audience and a broader interactivity which locates both performers and audience in a particular cultural moment. Spoken lines which—for that original audience—clearly echoed the phrasing of a prominent political figure will lose those associations as the culture evolves, and if the political echo was not so much in the actual lines as in an actor's style of delivery, say, what once seemed pointed may leave no textual traces by which the future might map the moment. Tracking the politics of the theatre is always about identifying the nature of an event and decoding the way all those involved in it (actors, crew, audience members, bystanders, etc.) respond to it. Unsurprisingly then, all assessments of political theatre must be provisional, plural, and contextual, so any consideration of what political theatre is must be rooted historically.

Most considerations of contemporary theatre's political valences begin with Bertolt Brecht (1898–1956), the playwright and dramatic theorist who most clearly dominated the twentieth century and whose influence continues to drive political theatre in the twenty-first century. Brecht was a German Marxist whose work spanned the Weimar Republic of the interwar years, Hitler's Nazi regime (during which he wrote largely from exile), and the post-war communist period of Soviet East Germany. He was influenced by the Russian symbolist director, Vsevolod Meyerhold, who sought a return to physical acting in the commedia dell'arte tradition (as opposed to the brand of modernist realism proposed by his contemporary and mentor, Stanislavsky) and by the German director, Erwin Piscator, whose politically driven productions utilized new theatrical technologies, such as cinematic projection. Brecht, in addition to using such technology, developed new dramatic and theatrical forms in tandem with a rethinking of the goals of theatre, the nature of the audience, and how that audience might engage their political reality through its experience of theatre. Brecht is a complex figure whose ideas evolved in the course of his career, and the fine points of his principles continue to be debated by critics who sometimes differ hotly over the precise meaning of crucial terms, but the general parameters of his aims and methodologies can be sketched with some clarity.[1]

Brecht saw the theatrical legacy of the nineteenth century as one which privileged emotion over intellect, spectacle over critical engagement, and bourgeois individualism over a sense of the collective. The audience member was encouraged to be passive to such an extent that he "hands the cloakroom attendant his brain along with his coat" (Bradley 3). Such audience members lose themselves in a completely contained theatrical fiction by which their feelings are manipulated and from which they emerge much the same as they went in, if purged of those emotional excesses Aristotle deemed dangerous to social stability. Such purgation (catharsis), Brecht saw as the bleeding off of important critical energies, energies which—in a different kind of theatre—might fuel political change for the betterment of society. This new kind of theatre must escape the restrictive category of the dramatic, to which Aristotle had consigned it, in which sentiment and melodrama acted upon the emotions alone, and straddle Aristotle's more intellectual and edifying artistic realm, the epic.

Brecht's notion of epic theatre—derived in part from Piscator who wrote about it in *The Political Theatre* (1929)—was an attempt to think of a mode of performance which would encourage audiences to reflect upon social structure and on the political means by which that structure was created and maintained. It aimed to contextualize character in terms of the larger social forces of economics, of ideology, and of war. Instead of losing themselves in the minor personal struggles of characters in a story, Brecht sought a theatre in which audiences would see themselves and their world in the theatre while retaining a critical distance from the experience. Audiences would be emotionally stirred, but not simply through empathic connection to characters, and their heightened emotional state would fuel the audience's thoughts and actions after the theatrical event was concluded.

In order to achieve this epic theatre, Brecht set about not just rethinking the content of dramatic scripts because the problem of subject matter was always, for him, suffused within a larger problem of theatrical form. The invisible fourth wall which defined the nineteenth-century proscenium stage led to, he believed, a species of containment which separated audience from performers in ways that rendered the emotional connection to the story and its characters trivial. Worse, such theatre did not merely miss an opportunity for political activism, it became complicit in the machinery of a state bent on presenting human activity as ultimately powerless in the alteration of the status quo. As such, the theatre as an institution had become a tool of the dominant, stripping art of its political edge and turning audiences into cattle. For Brecht, the solution was in encouraging audiences to resist associating with the fictional characters on stage so that they could see those characters in terms of a larger narrative rooted in the socio-political and economic landscape. Once prevented from total immersion in the logic of the story and empathic association with its characters, an audience would—through the resultant critical distance it retained—be empowered to recognize and analyse the larger and all-too-often obfuscated social, political, and economic forces at work inside the dramatic story, while also applying such analysis to the audience's own political reality.

Several strategies were employed to effect what he came to call *Verfremdungseffekte*, a term sometimes translated as the "estrangement" or, most commonly, "alienation" effect. This vexed term does not imply that the characters experience only a limited range of emotions, rather that their full emotional range is held up for scrutiny by an audience which has been encouraged to maintain a critical distance from the characters rather than associating with them as in conventional realist theatre. The characters are revealed as constructs on two levels, both inside and outside the play's internal logic. They are not actual people, but are the results of the labour of the dramatist, director, and acting company. Such a metatheatrical awareness of the character as construct is not an end in itself, however, but a device to reflect upon the social, political, and economic forces which shape both the character and the conditions from which the audience beholds that character. The audience are not alienated from the character in the sense of being repelled necessarily, rather seeing the character and his or her beliefs, aspirations, and actions, in the context of larger social forces. Instead of reacting merely emotionally to the characters, then, the audience are encouraged to maintain a distance which will allow them to process the character in context, analysing their behaviour intellectually as the microcosmic manifestation of broader economic and cultural issues. While the effect of *Verfremdung* is often to prevent an audience's total identification with the characters on stage, minimizing empathic connection, and destroying the totalizing illusion of realist theatre, these are means to an end, not ends in themselves. Rather *Verfremdung* is a process by which the substance of the play is "made strange" to the audience in ways engendering a different mental state which John J. White calls "a politicized critical distance" (White 117).

In further pursuit of a kind of theatre which did not completely draw audiences into the emotional frame of its fiction, the technical sleight of hand by which theatrical effects were rendered natural or invisible was abandoned on Brecht's stage. Stage lights—a comparatively new element of theatre technology at the time—were positioned where audiences could see them. Sets were made symbolic rather than realist. Backdrops included large-scale maps designed to show the play's action in the context of a broader social reality. Song, dance, and comedy were inserted into serious plays in ways foregrounding their artificial nature and subverting their tonal unity. Most controversially, acting style was rethought in terms other than the forms of realism and naturalism which had developed in the late nineteenth century. Actors were directed to utilize *gestus*—symbolic (non-realist) blocking or gesture used to emphasize a political point—and encouraged (contrary to most Stanislavskian models) not to associate with their character but to remain critically separate from them so that the audience would be encouraged to question their actions and choices, performative methodologies Brecht developed in part from early modern and Asian theatrical models. Actors used direct audience address to further disrupt the realism to which audiences had become accustomed and utilized a style of acting which was at least occasionally more presentationally artificial. Later in his career, Brecht moved away from the term 'epic' theatre and relied more (after Hegel) on the term 'dialectical' theatre, a term which shifts focus to the manner in which contrary positions are presented simultaneously in order to provoke active intellectual engagement on the part of the audience.[2]

Brecht was aware that theatre was potentially political not only in the sense of the content of plays but also in its mode of representation which, as Joe Kelleher says, is not only the representation of people who look and behave like us (the audience) but also the representation of a political delegate, "standing in for and standing up for us" (10). The result is the stirring up of conflict in the minds of the audience who, in turn, stand in for the larger social body in ways intended to raise awareness of and ultimately—however indirectly—to rectify social injustice and inequality. Tracy C. Davis's recent suggestion that the politically engaged audience is one which is moved not to sympathize but to think is a direct descendent of Brecht's, and her argument that such a position is achieved by standing aside from "the suffering of the righteous" in order to attain suitable critical distance echoes the goals of Brecht's alienation effect (Davis 154). It should be said that Brecht's impulse to create a politically self-aware audience who would be able to critique what they were experiencing inside (and outside) the theatre was a direct consequence of his work in the 1920s which was regularly interrupted or heckled by Nazi sympathizers. When it became clear that such people were to drive the country's national agenda, Brecht left Germany, spending most of the 1930s in Scandinavia until he could secure a visa to the United States, though he returned to Europe after falling foul of the House Committee on Un-American Activities (HUAC) in 1947. His final years in East Germany were lived in an increasingly vexed relationship with the Communist party government. In short, Brecht lived almost constantly at odds with authorities who were invested in total ideological orthodoxy and were prone to extreme repressive measures for those who would not comply. Such a position clearly framed his dissident view of how political theatre should function.

However much critics might quibble over the translation of *Verfremdungseffekte* as the "alienation" of the audience, arguing that the intent of the strategy is simply to produce a critical distance from the content of the play and its characters, intent must finally be subordinated to effect, and it has to be acknowledged that many audiences found the epic approach of Brecht and Piscator *unproductively* alienating. While their shows could be full of energy and humour as well as socio-political elucidation, the methodologies of epic or dialectical theatre remained marginal in terms of mainstream theatrical methodologies. Where politicized anti-realism stands shoulder to shoulder with the kind of familiar realism which offers emotional engagement without unsettling political and moral distancing, it is perhaps inevitable that some audiences will gravitate towards the latter, and persist in reading the former not as productive anti-realism, but as failed realism. While naturalism had been the driving force behind such politically adventurous and incendiary playwrights such as Ibsen and Chekhov, it also superficially resembled the "well-made play" which tended towards the predictable and comforting in its emotional purging. The epic/dialectical, by contrast was deliberately adversarial, discomforting, and designed to encourage analytical thought. It is unsurprising that, compelling though the work of Brecht and Piscator was, it never replaced its less politically deliberate rival and outside the Soviet world which once (albeit uneasily) championed their work, the epic/dialectical approach has become comparatively rare, even in the staging of Brecht's own plays.

Brecht's attitude to Shakespeare was complex. On the one hand, he saw in Shakespeare's dramaturgy the marks of a non-realist early modern stage craft which was, in certain respects, not dissimilar from (and was an influence upon) his own notion of epic theatre. The verse gave aesthetic shape and scale to utterance instead of presenting it simply as ordinary speech, and plays mixed radically different tonal matter (the mingling of kings and clowns so loathed by the eighteenth century). Dramatic action was interrupted by song and dance, characters addressed the audience directly, asides revealed a level of theatrical artifice within otherwise fairly naturalized scenes, and practices such as doubling, cross-gendered casting, and the use of (broadly speaking) contemporary dress all stood in opposition to the kind of fictionalized realism to which Brecht was so opposed. Furthermore, Brecht viewed the content of the plays themselves as extraordinarily rich and complex specifically in their articulation of political ideas. His study of the opening scene of *Coriolanus*, for instance, which takes the form of a dialogue with two other company members during the initial planning of a production of the play, shows a remarkable appreciation for the play's unsentimental and constructive realism in its representation of the ordinary people, their plight, and the way their struggle with the aristocracy is trumped by the threat of Volscian invasion. Where the opening scene can be read as a celebration of patrician values and a mockery of the plebeians, Brecht and his collaborators see a useful and sympathetic view of people caught in terrible and defining social circumstances:

P: The end of the scene is a little unsatisfactory.

B (BRECHT): In Shakespeare, you mean?

R: Possibly.

B: We'll note that sense of discomfort. But Shakespeare presumably thinks that war weakens the plebeians' position, and that seems to me splendidly realistic. Lovely stuff.

R: The wealth of events in a single short scene! Compare today's plays with their poverty of content!

P: The way in which exposition at the same time gives a rousing send-off to the plot!

R: The language in which the parable is told! The humor!

P: And the fact that it has no effect on the plebeians!

W: The plebeians native wit! Exchanges like "Agrippa: Will you undo yourselves? Citizen: We cannot, sir, we are undone already!"

R: The crystal clarity of Marcius's harangue! What an outsize character! And one who emerges as admirable while behaving in a way that I find beneath contempt!

B: And great and small conflicts all thrown on the scene at once: the unrest of the starving plebeians plus the war against their neighbours the Voscians; the plebeians hatred for Marcius, the people's enemy—plus his patriotism; the creation of the post of People's Tribune—plus Marcius's appointment to a leading role in the war. Well—how much of that do we see in the bourgeois theatre?

(Brecht 254–255)

Brecht does not look for a simple valorizing of the underclass, finding instead a complex articulation of social and economic factors usually kept out of theatre, factors which shape the characters and the main action of the play. It should not be surprising then, that when Brecht is dismissive of Shakespeare he is actually being dismissive of the way Shakespeare was conventionally read and staged, driven as such an attitude was by romantic and bourgeois suppositions Brecht did not see as intrinsic to the plays themselves. As the discussion of Coriolanus makes clear, Brecht's imagined production is both a reading of the play, and a reading *into* the play (264). Doc Rossi observes that for Brecht, "by presenting argument rather than suggestion, Shakespearean drama enables the audience to make a decision or 'cast a vote' one way or the other" (159). When Brecht dismisses American Shakespeare productions as "frightful" (Brecht 167), for example, he does so because of their stultifying speech making and the implied veneration of a cultural object. He sees improvization as central to Elizabethan play practice, something long since lost, experimentation with Shakespeare becoming instead a kind of "sacrilege" (172). In attacking the way the contemporary theatre presents Shakespeare, he identifies the problem of rooting audience response in empathy, on beautiful language and passages which provoke private imagination, things he considers largely incidental to the plays as written:

> Our theatres no longer have either the capacity or the wish to tell these stories, even the relatively recent ones of the great Shakespeare, at all clearly: i.e. to make the connection of events credible. And according to Aristotle—and we agree there—narrative is the soul of drama. We are more and more disturbed to see how crudely and carelessly men's life together is represented. (183)

This last sentence is crucial because it makes the connection between aesthetics and—via a form of naturalism—politics. Narrative form is about creating the social context for action and character ("how men's lives together is represented"), and for Brecht this—which is eminently present in Shakespeare's plays—has been lost not just in the writing of new works, but in the staging of Shakespeare's.

Not all theorists of political theatre seek an entirely new means of dramatic presentation. Some have specific goals which depend on a production using more conventional theatrical means to focus attention on a particular concern, rather than building a new model of the production/audience dynamic. One such is the actor, director, playwright, manager, and theorist Zygmunt Hubner, who was born in 1930 and raised in Poland during the Nazi occupation where he lived all his life, working in the theatre from 1955 to 1989, throughout the Soviet period. Like Brecht, Hubner saw value in the state's support of a politicized theatre, but he also ran foul of the restrictive mandates of the communist authorities and the Polish church, and his work in the 1980s was censored because of its implied critique of how martial law was used to crush anti-government protests. Since his work was confined to Poland, he is less well known than Brecht, less formative as an influence on other theatre theorists and practitioners, but his ideas are compelling nonetheless and he provides a fine instance of a theatre person for whom the world of his art and audience were inseparable from the political climate he saw defining them.[3] In his principal work on the subject, *Theatre and Politics* (1988), Hubner takes a large-scale view, tracking the issues through the course of western theatrical history from the ancient Greeks to the present, arguing that though material specificities change, the political struggles of the theatre have been ever with us.

Hubner made a distinction between ideology—the moral pursuit of a higher end—and politics—the expedient pursuit of power, concluding that if politics is the religion of the twentieth century, "it is a religion in which there is no place for saints" (5). Such a position problematizes the place of political theatre, itself a social institution which must engage with the political just to be relevant to life and must pursue a political agenda in order to be moral. As someone who has worked with state-funded theatres all his life, Hubner recognizes the precariousness of the theatre which, like a dog, must be cautious of biting the hand which feeds it, but still sees the very congregational nature of theatre to be that which increases its political power, its audience always being a gathering which might turn into a demonstration. The theatre is, he says, "both a Shakespearean mirror of the world and also a lens that focuses the rays of many suns. And a lens can start a fire" (6). How that fire gets lit is, for Hubner, not a matter of instituting new theatrical forms or "estranging" the audience from the subject matter staged before them, and he works with more conventional performance approaches to potentially subversive content. He is particularly concerned with undermining state censorship and advises an assortment of practical strategies including the delaying of a show's opening if it may incur the censor's wrath, to setting the most incendiary material to music. Hubner presents instances in which supposedly nervous actors "accidentally" delivered lines the censor had cut. He discusses the ways playwrights might make allusions instead of direct comparisons so that the audience (responding en masse) picks up topical connections the lone censor has missed. Playwrights might also take advantage of loopholes in censorship laws and practices, or set their clearly contemporary plays in a historical past which lends them a veil of unobjectionable venerability (62–65). In each case, Hubner assumes a kind of theatre which is set squarely against the totalitarian regime which ultimately controls it. His is a theatre that fights.

The flip side of censorship for Hubner, and one which is equally dangerous to the mission of art, is propaganda, something which is likely to taint any state-funded theatrical outfit. In this case, Hubner is not just thinking of the theatre funded by the Nazis or the Soviet communists, and he indicts the Comedie-Francaise, France's state-sponsored theatre, for its promotion of a version of what the nation is supposed to stand for (83–84). But as theatres can become propagandists for the state, so their very suitability to that role and their prior work as apologists for the state can make them equally well positioned for the dissemination of counter-cultural positions and ideologies, using its status "to challenge the powerful and become a theatre that fights" (103). Because of the practicalities of funding, Hubner's *Theatrum Militans* is dependent on the existence of a social class, national community or political grouping which both intends to seize power and sees the theatre as a viable tool in that struggle (106). In addition to countering the actions of the censor, theatre that fights might use various strategies including those more concerned with theatre as a community rather than the work of specific performances. Actors, for instance, might boycott participation in all state-sponsored radio and television programmes, they might sabotage propagandist productions or they might participate in active political agitation. The military dimension of this last point is clear from Hubner's description of what he calls agitational theatre:

> In attempting to characterize... the stylistic diversity of propagandistic theatre, I stressed its baroque tendency to employ a rich variety of means. Agitational theatre, although poorer by its very nature, does not in the least exclude scenic effect, but whereas the propagandistic effect is to dazzle and arouse awe, agitation must surprise and startle. Agitation is a poster: it works by shock, unexpected shortcuts, exaggeration, sharpness of outline, legibility. The intellectual content must be easily assimilated, and the emotional reactions of the spectator spontaneous. Agitation is also a battle, and thus words like blow, charge, attack, encirclement, which come from military terminology, are quite appropriate in this case. The opponent must be put out of action and defeated at all cost. This can be accomplished by unmasking his real and obviously treacherous and underhanded machinations and by ridiculing his illusory might. (139)

It is in pursuit of this last point that theatre, Hubner says, most often uses oversized masks and puppetry, anachronistic scenic elements, and film, all of which can be used to lay bare the target of the theatre's critique, and which often reveal origins in the carnival world of the fairground and other places on the fringes of order and regimented society. Like Brecht, Hubner sees the key to much agitational theatre as the destruction of the fourth wall so that the actors and audiences see and recognize each other instead of being trapped within the fiction of the bourgeois theatre.

Hubner saw Shakespeare's plays in the terms espoused by fellow Polish radical, Jan Kott, for whom the plays had an urgent political relevance, particularly the way they threw light on the "Grand mechanism of history" (Hubner 55), though Hubner did not see the plays as intrinsically the stuff of theatre that fights. He discusses the way Tsarist Russia banned clearly incendiary plays such as *Macbeth* and *Richard III*, while plays as wide ranging as *Antony and Cleopatra* and *A Midsummer Night's Dream* were censored in Poland, but he notes that the banning of *King Lear* in England in 1817 occurred because the royal madness in the play was looking increasingly topical given the mental condition of George III (56). The *perception* of subversion by its audience might be as potent as subversion intended by the playwright or theatre company, and in some cases the moment of staging might draw on potentially subversive ideas within a play which, in the current political moment, become incendiary. This, he implies, was the case in the staging by Shakespeare's company of *Richard II* on the eve of the Essex rebellion in 1601 (153–155). For Hubner, Shakespeare was not a radical writer who called explicitly for—for instance—the abolition of monarchy, rather being the kind of author whose complex work lent itself to politically provocative theatre which, in the right circumstances, might become more aggressively subversive (105).

Despite Hubner's wealth of historical exemplar from all over western theatre, his notion of the kind of political struggle in which the theatre is engaged is shaped entirely by his Polish context and the totalitarian regimes under which he worked. For other theorists and practitioners whose states have different relationships with the theatre, their sense of purpose and methodology is quite different. For Ric Knowles, for instance, such social and material differences are central to a way of thinking about political theatre which must consider theatrical meaning as generated by three separate but interconnected constituent parts: the performance, the conditions of production, and the conditions of reception (Knowles 19). Like W.B. Worthen and other recent theorists of theatrical practice, Knowles seeks to apply the intellectual rigour discovered by the late twentieth-century theoretical movements to the workings of live theatre, overturning some of the familiar naiveties about how audiences read performance and therefore how meaning is made on stage. Knowles establishes a theoretical self-consciousness for how theatre produces meaning not simply in terms of the script performed, the look of the set and costumes or the performances of the actors, but by examining all factors which influence both the shaping of the production (conscious and otherwise) and the shaping of the reception of each individual performance. He calls this method "materialist semiotics," a process by which the critic might scrutinize all the signs through which theatre creates meaning but to the list of what is done (usually) deliberately by a company he adds everything which has an effect on how an audience might process what it is seeing. This includes, for instance, a consideration of the differences between the cultural moment (in both geographical and temporal terms) in which a production is generated and that in which it is received. So the discrepancy between the last two of his three key elements (the conditions of production and the conditions of reception) means that a touring production which goes unaltered in terms of what happens on stage (the performance "itself") can have radically different political effects—meanings—when it transfers from, say, London's Old Vic theatre to the Alex in Toronto (166–168).[4]

Knowles is as interested in the driving concerns about who sanctions theatrical production, who finances it, as is Hubner, but because Knowles's primary focus is not Soviet Poland but twentieth- and twenty-first century Britain, the United States and—especially—Canada, the answers are more complex. Such answers are, however, crucial to assessing that most tricky and elusive element of theatrical production, its effect, particularly in the case of political theatre where it is fair to ask what a show actually *does*. How, for instance, might the leftist rhetoric of a director or company manager be subverted by the source of their funding as part of a purely capitalist corporation? How might said company's claims to speak for an under class be problematized by the fact that the show played only in well-heeled locations charging exorbitant ticket prices, never venturing into those regions whose concerns they were supposedly representing? How might audience response be tracked, and what does it suggest if the production's radical politics were somehow missed by an audience who thought (based perhaps on their own cultural location) they were experiencing something else entirely because they did not recognize a particular culturally marked element such as an actor's dialect or signature piece of clothing? In raising these questions, Knowles counters the all-too common universalist assumption that theatrical meaning is reducible to the contents of the script and directorial (or company) "choices," as if concerns about venue, funding and the like are mere "accidentals of historical and cultural context" (9) which have no bearing on the production's final semantic weight. Such traditional approaches to how theatre makes meaning efface "significant cultural and material differences based on such things as national, political, cultural, and geographical location, together with class, race, ethnicity, gender and sexuality" (10). Each production can thus be identified on a continuum in which one end represents the transgressive and transformative potential of the art object, while the other represents the interests and ideology of the dominant social order. The unseen conditions of production and reception serve as the production's "political unconscious, speaking through the performance text whatever its manifest content or intent" (10). In short, the material conditions by which a production is generated and staged may actively subvert and trump the apparent political content of the production itself. We must therefore be alert to such "accidentals" before pronouncing on the production's political nature and effect, all of which must finally be provisional, local, and limited to a sense of the range of meanings open to individual audience members, not a definitive statement about what a production "meant" (21). For Knowles, theatre is not a broadcast of meaning but a negotiation between performers and audiences, both of which are informed by factors not clearly visible on stage. In this latter category, we must therefore consider the methods and assumptions behind specific kinds of theatre training—the assumptions inculcated into actors, directors, designers, and so forth—company structure and organization, the nature and location of physical theatrical buildings and performance spaces, as well as the specifics of relevant legislation, of company economics and payment. All are finally relevant in the way a production makes meaning in general and political meaning in particular.

Knowles's attitude to Shakespeare, like Hubner's, is thus provisional, insisting that the political valences of a production include and are dependent on the material, fiscal and demographic conditions of the entire performative moment. In an extended consideration of the 1993 season at Ontario's Stratford Festival, Knowles contextualizes the productions of *Antony and Cleopatra*, *A Midsummer Night's Dream* and *King John* in ways going beyond individual actor choices, costuming, soundscape, and other aspects of the directorial "concept," to include not just the architecture of the playing spaces but their economic and cultural underpinnings, scrutinizing at what points the appearance of subversion might actually provoke or unsettle—rather than merely titillate—its largely affluent audience. Articulating and extending some of Hubner's assumptions, Knowles concludes thus:

> No production of Shakespeare can be assessed outside of the material context within and through which it is produced, any more can the production of the scripts themselves. At Stratford, Ontario in 1993, where even more than at most theatres the institutional context tended to function with remarkable directness as an Ideological State Apparatus, funded by government and corporate grants and catering to an audience it constructed as monolithic, the production of Shakespeare is necessarily the reproduction of a complex and shifting but nevertheless conservative, affirmative culture, endorsed by the appropriated, high cultural image of a universalist "Bard of Avon". (127–128)

It need not, Knowles suggests, be so, but it takes more than a few hip costumes and punked-up hairstyles to make Shakespeare radical, and such things can be used to disguise productions which are either weakly apolitical or deeply conservative. The marriage of state- and corporate-sponsored theatre with an author whose works have been used to champion all manners of western hegemonic assumptions requires particular vigilance on the part of both theatre practitioners and critics, an idea to which I return in Chapter 2.

Knowles is a theorist and critic rather than a theatre practitioner, but he shares assumptions about the material conditions surrounding theatre, its audience, and its meanings with one of the most important practitioners of recent political theatre, the Brazilian founder of the Theatre of the Oppressed, Augusto Boal (1931–2009). On account of his early activism and Marxist sympathies, Boal was captured, tortured, and exiled for 15 years by the right-wing military dictatorship which governed Brazil, but on his return, in 1986, he persisted in his work for human rights, initiating a new phase of his work (The Legislative Theatre), and becoming a city councillor for Rio de Janeiro. Instead of targeting large-scale political issues through conventional drama, Boal's core method involves giving voice to his audience and building theatre around their own concerns and issues, particularly for the disenfranchised, the poor and the otherwise marginalized elements of society. His goal was to free the audience from an oppressive theatrical model which renders them passive, instead giving them the space and prompt to self-expression and activism which are intended to generate social liberation. As such he was influenced by his friend and compatriot, Paulo Freire, the educational theorist. Freire seeks to empower the learners rather than treat them as vessels whose function is to merely receive uncritically the information which is decanted into them by a dominant social order. Instead of creating a monolithic theatre in the conventional sense, Boal's legislative theatre worked on the building of theatrical groups within existing communities among the politically and economically oppressed. For Boal, the "spect-actors" (the term he used to identify the active audience members) are energized through a consideration of their own bodies, the bodies of performers, and their sense of larger "bodies"—collectives or groups (as in student body), and learning to use those bodies through expressive theatricality in political discourse. In a demonstration of Boal's democratizing politics and socialist sensibilities, participants utilized a blend of memory and imagination "to reinvent the past and to invent the future" in ways which "systematize...potentialities and render them accessible to use by anyone and everyone" (*Legislative Theatre* 7). Like Brecht before him, Boal sees theatre not as mere entertainment in the bourgeois mode but as a tool for socio-political enlightenment ("consciousness raising" in the Marxist sense) and material change.

The specifics of how the spect-actor principle works in practice vary, but one instance is a technique known as simultaneous dramaturgy; a play will be performed up to a particular moment of crisis, a moment of decision by one of the characters, say, when the performance will stop and the audience will be asked their opinion. Based on what the actors are told, they will then improvise the conclusion of the play. The device is designed to give a voice to people who, in other parts of their lives, feel that they have none, and in some forms the audience members' suggestions are played out by the audience themselves who are invited to take over key roles in the production. In the "forum theatre" model, the scripted play which is the core of the production centres on a particularly oppressive dynamic—the representation of an abusive marriage, for instance, or an exploitative work environment—and ends without a resolution of the key problem. The play is then restaged, and the audience can stop the action at any point, inserting themselves into the role of the oppressed to try and change the course of the action. When a satisfactory conclusion is reached, the audience are then invited to become the oppressors so as to get them to understand all sides and motivations involved, the goal being finally dialectical rather than the teaching of lessons or solutions. When the audience encounters similar situations in real life, they will—Boal says—have the benefit of having already rehearsed the scene, an advantage which will, it is hoped, render them quicker to recognize possible solutions and be more active in effecting them. This methodology formed the heart of Boal's legislative theatre in which, as a councilman, he was able to use this improvizational and inclusive approach in the debating and finally passing of actual legislation. In each case, Boal believed that the spec-actor develops a more critical investment in the issue being explored through active participation than he or she would if functioning solely as an audience member to a piece of politically inflected theatre.

Throughout his life Boal was fascinated by Shakespeare, by the scale of his language and by his consciousness of social reality and its economic underpinnings. He read *Hamlet*, for instance, as a play which emerged from the transition taking place between the feudal and the bourgeois, Old Hamlet standing for the former and Claudius for the latter. Hamlet's existential crisis is thus precipitated by the title character wrestling with the sense that he is somehow both, a man divided between social systems whose tragedy is that his answer to the question of whether to be or not to be is that he must somehow do both.

> Hamlet... is the father and the uncle. He just does not know how to be himself. He does not recognise in himself his other I. Which of the two is "Hamlet"? Both. I am a specialist in this dichotomy....
> (*Hamlet and the Baker's Son* 130)

Hamlet's divided self which might be read in romantic or Freudian terms thus turns on a sense of social context and the attendant models of selfhood which stem from each. The dichotomy which Boal recognizes in himself (and which is echoed by the balanced title of the autobiography from which I have quoted) is thus a conflict between emergent power and older values which were crumbling, though "the latter contains the former, and the former has residues of the latter" (143). In Shakespeare, Boal found characters who were socially and historically enmeshed, characters who spoke out of their condition and who—within the fiction of the play and through the form of its original theatrical practice—*interacted* with each other and with their audience. This became a fundamental idea for his Theatre of the Oppressed. Moreover, Shakespeare, like Cervantes and other "classics," contributed to Boal's sense of play as metaphor (315) and to his conviction that linguistic articulation—"words, words, words"—was the wellspring of life, when living itself was not (348).

If there is a logical progression from Knowles to Boal, it is a progression which recognizes the influence of the material on theatrical meaning in ways which push the domain of political theatre outside the conventional realm of the dramatic and into the performative. Boal's theatre of the oppressed rethinks what theatre buildings are and what plays might be in the practitioner's response to that recognition of the material theatre made both by Knowles and, in different terms, by Hubner, as rooted in larger social forces, particularly in economics. Boal's attempt to escape the constraints of a theatre moulded by state power, by finance, and by the nature of theatre as both a physical and ideological space within high culture presses him to engage audiences differently. Plays are rescripted (or de-scripted), audiences are rendered active participants, performance spaces are found, or built far from the theatre districts, and in the process a political radicalism is engineered less through theatre in the traditional sense than through a notion of performance which is broader and more idiosyncratic. The logic of such a movement is made theoretically explicit in the work of Baz Kershaw, for whom " 'performance beyond theatre' is a more fruitful realm for radicalism than performance in theatre" (16).

Kershaw considers the nature of political theatre through the lenses of the modern and the postmodern, collapsing that binary and seeking for ways to rediscover a form of radical theatre in the increasingly performative world of contemporary democratic capitalism. Kershaw floats first Richard Schechner's analogy of the traditional (modernist) theatre becoming "the string quartet of the twenty first century: a beloved but extremely limited genre, a subdivision of performance" (14), then David George's version of (postmodern) performance as "limitless" in its capacity to discover, provoke, and—in some senses—*be* everything. At the root of some of these concerns about what "theatre" is are notions we saw underlying Brecht's unease with the bourgeois theatre of the nineteenth century, which a more generalized sense of "performance" seeks to reform. This reformation involves moving outside traditional theatre buildings and their physicalizing of institutionalized privilege, and an approach to theatricality which goes beyond conventional notions of form, of audience, and of script. Though Kershaw is careful to complicate this sketch, the movement from theatre to performance is generally one "from fixity to flexibility, from cohesion to fragmentation, from hierarchy to equality, from unity to plurality, from culture to multi-cultures and so on" (15). Yet though Kershaw does see "performance beyond theatre" as likely to generate the most potent political meanings, he sees both the traditional theatre and the more inclusive category of performance as participating in each other, crossing paradigms because of the way the larger performative society evolves.

Kershaw prefers the term "radical" to "political" in terms of performance, not just because the old assumption that leftist theatre is political while conservative theatre isn't is clearly problematic but because politics has now become so ubiquitous and recognizable in the representation or negotiation of any issue of social power (material or ideological) that the term "political theatre" is almost tautological. Radical performance, by contrast, is one which is politically neutral (associated with neither the right nor the left), asserting only the need for, as Raymond Williams puts it "vigorous and fundamental change" (18). For Kershaw, radical performance "gestures beyond all forms of the dogmatic, towards kinds of freedom that currently cannot be envisaged," though he also interrogates the ways that the very fluidity of postmodernism actually limits creative radicalism. The postmodern has deconstructed old hierarchies and assumptions, but in the process it has also brought "the death of community, the loss of agency, the end of history, even the demise of meaning in the wholesale rejection of anything that smacks of ontological and epistemological certainty."

Kershaw's solution is to advocate for forms of radical performance which reach beyond "existing systems of formalised power" through transgressive or transcendent performances which do not so much represent freedom as produce it in the performative moment (19). Kershaw's critique of the traditional theatre is threefold and grounded expressly in a specifically late twentieth-century British incarnation. First, he argues that theatre reinforces certain modes of perception/reception which are derived from the larger social structure, specifically consumerism and commodification. Second, he targets the theatre's complicity in the formation of social categories such as gender, race, class, and age. Third, he says that theatre buildings partake of "spatial indoctrination" to instil normative social values (31–32). Most damning of all, Kershaw concludes that "increasingly theatre has become a social institution from which equality and mutual exchange—the practice of citizenship through common critique, say—is all but banished" (32). It should be pointed out that the theatre Kershaw is targeting primarily is that of the greatest mass appeal and highest profit margins, internationally travelling musicals like *Cats, The Phantom of the Opera*, and, especially, *Miss Saigon*, which he subjects to a blistering critique of orientalism. Such a theatrical model, as Kershaw points out, squares nicely with what Brecht called "culinary" theatre, in which the gullible audience is plied with sensory indulgence in ways that disarm their critique of the deeply conservative core of the fare consumed (52).

As can be inferred from these statements, and contrary to the other critics I have surveyed thus far, Kershaw has little interest in conventional productions of Shakespeare, and this raises a concern which is the driving force behind Chapter 2. The last century of dramatic theory and practice, as the above suggests, is a pattern of theorists and practitioners struggling to make political meaning—and largely radical, in Kershaw's sense—political meaning out of an institution they assume to be conservative, limiting—even restrictive—and invested in the social politics of the status quo. The forms of those larger social pressures vary according to period and cultural locale (Victorian bourgeois, Nazi, Soviet communist, or late twentieth-century global capitalism), but the pattern is consistent. Theatre gets co-opted by the state, by corporations, and by the dominant hegemony. The only clear ways to escape the paradigm are through the reinvention of the theatrical form itself, breaking down old ideas about the passive spectator through disruption, even shocking disruption of that form through radical dramaturgy, whether through non-naturalist acting a la Brecht or through the incorporation of audience response a la Boal. These approaches go beyond the representation of political content and demand a reconceptualization of what theatre is, a reconceptualization which, in Kershaw's terms, pushes further into a mode of radical performance which is figuratively and often literally outside the conventional theatre.

Shakespeare and, for that matter, other conventional drama, does not easily fit such a radical model, requiring as we might assume it does, a known script delivered to a fixed and recognizably non-interactive audience within a conventional theatre building. Such theatre is, in Benjamin Bennett's sense, transitive, because it has an object which is being presented (a play which can exist outside performance as literary text), while radical performance is—or at least claims to be—in some senses intransitive, having no prior object to play beyond what is constructed in the performative moment (Bennett 6). Can transitive theatre like Shakespeare ever escape containment by the so-called establishment, and if not must such production always merely serve the ideological position and structure of that establishment? To answer in the affirmative may seem hopeful at best, but we must not lose sight of one of the other dominant points raised by the aforementioned critics and theorists concerning the locational specificity of performance and the semiotic instability of its communicative form. Both of these argue against the overview as an approach to assessing theatrical meaning, inviting us rather to consider a complex nexus of forces which shape those myriad meanings for the individual audience member. These are notoriously difficult to track and harder still to finally evaluate, but they present opportunities for analysis where audience members escape even the most conservative of theatrical paradigms. Does traditional theatre necessarily reproduce such paradigms? Perhaps in the abstract, but even traditional theatre must finally be considered on a case by case basis in which we evaluate everything from ticket prices and seat configuration to the current cultural and political climate and the audience demographic as well as assessing the overt content of the play and the mode of presentation by the company, bearing in mind that even that which a play does explicitly is open to interpretation. After all, even Kershaw's critical reading of the orientalist *Miss Saigon* was, in some ways, engendered by the production itself; individual audience members will find a range of disparate, even contradictory meanings in the same performance, and the political content of such meanings is valid even if it is not intended by the production's company. Reception is all. We must allow for political readings to emerge from traditional theatre and not only when the audience member, like Kershaw at *Miss Saigon*, is reading wilfully against the grain of the production.

Such a concession props the door for other kinds of political readings facilitated by productions of traditional theatre which are able to evade some elements of that totalizing, conservative model theorists invoke. The political valences of a production of Shakespeare alter when the company takes their show on the road, particularly if they play for radically different audiences than are their usual: school children, say, prisoners, or the socially disadvantaged. The production may still (and perhaps more insidiously) reinforce certain conservative social and political principles in the minds of its audience, but it may generate entirely different ideas and energies. Whether those are intended by the company, its financers or its larger cultural investments are finally as irrelevant as are any statements of authorial intentionality to the production of meaning. If an audience member perceives radical politics in a production funded by the state or a massive multinational corporation, those facts sit somewhat uneasily together, but the irony does not necessarily puncture the audience's perception, particularly if the impression that audience takes away feeds other kinds of political action elsewhere.

The political impact of conventional theatre is likely to be less immediate and—ironically—less dramatic than that of radical performance though it might be argued that the agitprop of such performance is often more a manifestation of political feeling which is already extant than it is the generator of such feeling. The "audiences" and "performers" who flocked to the Berlin wall did not do so out of a conscious impulse to perform or witness a performance except in so far as the mood surrounding the performative event promised some sort of tipping point. That that point took a performative shape derived as much, as Kershaw points out, from liturgical and anthropological impulses as they did from the theatrical (110–111), and one might argue that such radical performance preaches to the choir: giving vent to a general feeling rather than creating it.

Unless one is caught unawares by a piece of performance as in the flash mob form where a theatrical event is concealed to the moment it breaks out in a public place, most people go to protest performance for expressly political reasons. By contrast, most people (and clearly I'm speculating here) go to conventional theatre for other reasons, even when the subject matter is political. This is because theatre is generally discursive, even when the audience is not invited to participate in the exchange, because it (again, generally) involves multiple voices and therefore the presentation of differing opinion. Such theatre can, of course, be polemic just as radical performance can be discursive, but it seems reasonable to think that conventional theatre which is also political is more about changing minds than it is about effecting action. It is less radical, no doubt, less direct in its ambition, but in cultures like Britain and particularly the United States it has the advantage of being part of a larger political conversation and is less easily dismissed as mere fringe activism. Its effects are less visible, less easily accessible than that of a rally which overturns statues or dumps tea into the river, but in not chasing the two minute spot on the television news, they might be allowed more substance. Perhaps, as with all things to do with the theatre, the proof is in the specifics of the pudding.

Bennett argues that the potential radicalism of drama (not simply of performance) lies in the way it necessarily problematizes the inherently conservative tendency of the literary. "Drama," he says, "by way of its indissoluble association with the brute materiality of theatre, disrupts fundamentally, and opens to the possibility of revolution, the otherwise at least potentially closed systems of Western literature" (8). By this he does not mean that either the theatre as an institution or any individual performance is inherently revolutionary in direct political terms but that drama destabilizes genre which is necessarily conservative as an a priori limit on interpretation and therefore on meaning. Genre confines a work's range of meanings and, even where its rules are broken, frames what such transgression means by existing before hand. The result is what Bennett calls a conservative "tendency" in literature, which drama evades by not relying solely on literary signification but on the material conditions which shape the theatrical and which therefore root it in social reality. As such, even the work of conservative dramatists becomes revolutionary in performance, according to Bennett, because "all theater—whether it will or no—is revolutionary theater" (48). While Bakhtin's notion of heteroglossia (the overlapping of multiple voices in ways generating conflict and subverting univocal meaning) is *perceivable* in the novel, it is the fundamental state of theatrical drama in which the dialogue of the text is only the beginning of the meanings which will be generated in performance (52). A given line can be delivered any number of ways by an actor, and the meanings of the moment will necessarily be shaped by factors which have no origin in the text per se: the special arrangement of characters, their costume, look, gesture, the nature of the light on the stage and so on. Drama is not stable, its meanings not limited by the word on the page. Rather it is essentially disruptive to the idea of the literary.

In the context of what I have already cited from other critics, Bennett's position may seem rather abstract to be of real use, but it is clear that his core principle is at work in those critics who demand a more explicitly political dimension to the theatrical effect. Brecht, clearly, was trying to augment what Bennett sees as theatre's inherently heteroglossic nature by shattering familiar forms which pressed the dramatic into something we might call the literary on stage. Knowles sees the material theatre—its structures, its funding streams, the social pressures on its audience— as factors finally determining a heteroglossic function at odds not just with the literary, but with elements of the theatrical itself. Boal expands the theatre's heteroglossic function by breaking the fourth wall entirely and making the resultant performance a collaboration which empowers the audience. Kershaw sees an intransitive mode of performance which escapes the conditions of neocapitalism as a taking back of theatre's discoursive and subversive elements from an institution too tied to larger socio-political and economic structures. In each case, these critics and practitioners are seeking to exploit the potentially subversive elements of Bennett's brutely material theatre against the constraints of the literary and, by extension, the establishment. If we concede that such a thing is possible, that subversive political energies and ideas can be generated even by the traditionally defined transitive theatre, what is the place of that supremely literary object, the Shakespearean play? Can what culture persists in identifying with the dread honorific "The Bard" ever be anything other than the mouthpiece of the establishment or, as many of the critics discussed here assume, does such an honorific become meaningless in the material conditions of production, and what political possibilities at the local level are then made possible by staging Shakespeare?

2
The Curious Case of Mr Shakespeare

As Chapter 1 suggests, there can be no innate paradox between the notion of radical theatre and Shakespearean production where people like Brecht, Boal, and Knowles see Shakespeare's plays, their original performance conditions and their capacity for contemporary deployment as potentially subversive, but the matter remains vexed. For Brecht, utilizing Shakespeare in the pursuit of an epic or dialectical theatre requires a stripping of Shakespeare's bourgeois and romantic accretions, a return to the non-realist origins of his theatre practice and an extension of his latent interests in representing the populace, but this is no mean task and questions remain about the extent to which a production can escape Shakespeare's high cultural baggage. After all, if theatre as an institution is often bound to cultural hegemony and the ideological conformity that implies, what chance of escaping that paradigm has an author whose work is pre-eminently enshrined in the Western cultural hierarchy? Is it impossible for Shakespeare on stage to be truly radical? While political interrogation of the plays has become central to literary study, particularly in terms of the triumvirate of cultural studies—gender, race, and class—identity politics in performance is harder to see in conventional productions, partly because of the way macro concerns tend to get individuated in the body of the actor, so that a more abstract debate about the place of women, for instance, tends to play as a psychological study of a single character. Even when productions take a more political tack, it might be asked whether they can overcome the audience's assumptions about what Shakespeare is and represents, or whether such a production can realistically reach more than a financially and educationally privileged elite. Further, if Shakespeare can be brought to other audiences, is that necessarily a good thing, or does it serve only to evangelize a dominant world view which creates a deeper sense of cultural alienation in the less traditional audience? Where productions modulate their text to accommodate such audiences, to what extent are they still "doing Shakespeare," and does such modulation suggest that the only way to render the plays politically effective is to virtually throw them out and start over?

I have no interest in branding all Shakespeare productions as inherently conservative, committed as I am to a specifically local sense of what theatre is rather than to macro statements. It is the conviction of this book that Shakespeare on the stage can be politically both instructive and subversive, even if it cannot fully escape the exclusive mechanisms of both Shakespeare and the theatre in culture, even if its political victories are minor and incremental. Theatre—Shakespearean or otherwise—does not, cannot, create utopia by itself, but then neither does anything else. Assessing the political valences of Shakespeare on stage must finally take place at the level of the particular. Before we get to such specifics, however, let us consider the case in broader terms.

In order to wrestle with any idea of Shakespeare as being an Establishment monolith or emblem of an oppressive "high" or simply—but problematically—normative culture, it is helpful to first consider the position of those who might be seen to be at odds with such an Establishment not simply because of ideological difference but because of an alienation which acts at the most basic level of selfhood and subjectivity. To do so, and in preparation for the specifics of Chapter 3, I explore what has come to be called "identity politics" as a corollary to the largely class-rooted politics of Chapter 1.

Identity politics grows out of ideas about the social oppression of individuals and groups who feel marginalized as a consequence of elements they consider fundamental to their identity: their gender, for instance, their race or ethnicity, their sexual orientation. Each of these subsets is distinctly different and each contains a range of opinion and agenda, though all share a sense of political identity emerging from shared experience. Though rooted in earlier writings, most were first expressly articulated as the politics of identity in the late twentieth century and hinge on the notion that much which was formerly considered absolute or essential is in fact the product of social forces, economics, and ideological pressures. Ideas and behavioural practices emerging from the dominant (usually white, heterosexual, and male) thus shape not only ideas about those outside that dominant, such as women or members of other races, but also coercive behavioural models and notions of self.

Simone de Beauvoir's landmark *The Second Sex*, for instance, argued that women were made rather than born and that the process of making was largely a conforming to controlling male desires and expectations by which patriarchy restricted and devalued women, often through the process of mystification. As Judith Butler subsequently clarified, for de Beauvoir the dominant mark of the female is the socially constructed category of gender, not the seemingly absolute biological category of sex, and that the body itself is in fact a construction because it cannot be understood (or manipulated or overwritten) except through social context:

> The notion that there might be a "truth" of sex, as Foucault ironically terms it, is produced precisely through the regulatory practices that generate coherent identities through the matrix of coherent gender norms. The heterosexualization of desire requires and institutes the production of "male" and "female". The cultural matrix through which gender identity has become intelligible requires that certain kids of "identities" cannot "exist"—that is, those in which gender does not follow from sex.
>
> (Atkins 283)

Clearly such philosophical deconstruction of what might otherwise be considered ontological, essential, or "natural" has significant political consequences for notions of gendered identity and its implications for thought and behaviour, though the nature of those implications varies according to the particular form of feminism the critics enact. For Adrienne Rich, to take a range of views on sexuality, heterosexuality is a politicized institution whose nature is coercive, and for Andrea Dworkin, pornography is an engine of patriarchal oppression designed to control through debasement, while Carol Vance seeks a politics "that resists deprivation and supports pleasure" and, fighting the notion that the structures of heterosexuality are essentially debilitating for women, insists that "women are sexual subjects, sexual actors, sexual agents" (Kemp and Squires 320–335). Whether critics and thinkers identify themselves as liberal, Marxist, radical, socialist, womanist, or other subsets of feminist thought affects their philosophy and political goals, but they share the notion that feminism concerns large-scale cultural issues of identity more than it does the notion of equality with men. Rather, feminism is, as Sally J. Scholz says, "a critical project" which "looks at all aspects of life to identify those elements which might be oppressive and suggests alternatives" (1). On stage, feminist critics and theatre practitioners often strive to expose gender as a construct, sometimes (as in critics such as Elin Diamond or playwrights like Caryl Churchill) utilizing a form of Brechtian "alienation" in the representation and analysis of sex/gender (through cross-gendered casting, for instance) in ways which make the audience aware of gender as a socially deployed and restrictive category. Jill Dolan seeks not just to demystify the supposed universality of the dominant spectator (and thus reinterrogate those aspects of gender which, though constructs, tend to get "naturalized" by appeal to that dominant spectator) but to reclaim new versions of, for instance, female sexuality through performative agency.[1]

The impulse of identity politics to seek to break down the essentialism at the heart of hegemonic discourse, to reclaim versions of identity outside the highly restrictive assumptions of the dominant order, is a useful method for rethinking race and ethnicity. As with matters of gender, the defining position in Western culture has come from the white, male-dominant order and, until recently, has gone largely unchallenged in mainstream culture, so that racist stereotypes and assumptions continue to affect not only the way the dominant sees minorities, but also the way minorities see themselves. As with feminist theory, the task of critics who write about race, ethnicity, and multiculturalism is to expose the constructs of race, to strip it of its biological essentialism, and to analyse the way race and ethnicity affect individuals and communities. In *Orientalism*, for instance, Edward Said traces the way the West has defined the East as Other in ways serving imperial political and economic ends and which continue to prevent that East's self-definition, though his project is also a rigorous attack on those very notions of discrete races and cultures which are so central to hegemonic discourse and cultural history.[2]

Similar strategies have been deployed by African American critics such as Henry Louis Gates whose *Signifying Monkey* was an attempt to read African American literature through the black vernacular tradition and thus to let African American literature "speak for itself about its nature and various functions, rather than to read it, or analyse it, in terms of theories borrowed whole from other traditions, appropriated from without" (Gates xix). As with feminist criticism, the critical project (to use Scholz's phrase) is about the analysis and redefinition of people and their culture who have traditionally been defined largely as Other to and by the white, male-dominant order.[3]

The way identity politics scrutinizes assumptions about biology as a blind for political and economic manipulation in matters of gender and race makes it similarly useful in the analysis of and advocacy for issues of sexual preference and orientation. Outside the normative fictions of Western hegemonic discourse, sexual identity escapes the supposedly determinative factors of biology, facilitating a critical space for the analysis of gay, lesbian, queer, or transgendered identity which avoids the morally laden discursive frames of the past. David Savran's essay collection, whose queer theory of American theatre is also expressly Marxist, focuses on abjection: "Most frequently, abjection is a result of processes of normalization, for orthodoxy defines itself only by constructing a heretical Other" (x). Savran puts his finger on an assumption at the heart of identity politics that the dominant creates all which it stands against in order to clarify and further its own sense of self, usually in ways designed to marginalize—or demonize—all which it is not.

So where does this leave Shakespeare? No figure in literary or theatrical history has been more clearly identified with that dominant order against which identity politics sets itself. Shakespeare's plays not only wrote women and non-Caucasian races in ways which have, arguably, furthered stereotypical assumptions about both but also enacted them in the theatre at a time when neither women nor non-white actors could appear on stage. Even if politically driven theatre practitioners such as Brecht or Boal could find Shakespeare comparatively easy to assimilate into their various forms of radical or subversive theatre, the challenge to Shakespeare from critics invested in identity politics seems on the face of it daunting indeed. Brecht and Boal were looking at Shakespeare as a study in class-based politics, and one who—at least for Brecht—grew out of a theatre which in some ways resembled his own versions of epic or dialectical practice. For some identity critics, Shakespeare may well be—to put it starkly—the enemy.

Yet identity politics has had a massive effect on how we read and study Shakespeare since the 1970s, so that reading Shakespeare from the margins has become—ironically—the dominant mode in which higher education navigates the plays. Shakespeare's political nature can be tracked in various ways, most simply perhaps, in terms of the plays' political content on the one hand and their political application on the other, and though these two clearly inform each other it is helpful to consider them separately, beginning with the former. Since the late 1970s, the dominant mode in which Shakespeare is studied and taught, particularly at the university level, is one which has moved away from older concerns with aesthetics, with a brand of character-centred criticism, and with so-called universal themes, becoming instead more politically inflected. In some cases such inflection has aligned the plays and their author with the dominant social order, while others take the opposite position, arguing that the plays pick at and unravel the logic of that larger social order to the point of being revolutionary at least in terms of the ideas at work, if not promoting outright rebellion. Those critics who assume the plays finally endorse the cultural hegemony (often grouped together as New Historicists) argue that any apparent subversion within the plays is finally contained within a reinscription of the society's dominant values, that the theatre itself functions to permit the articulation of such dangerous ideas in a safe and non-threatening environment, from which the audience leave confirmed in their citizenry and reinvested in the ideology of the state.[4] Such a position supports normative readings of gender, ethnicity, class structure, monarchy, religious discourse, and all other major ideological components of life. Other critics (often called Cultural Materialists) take the subversive elements within the plays more seriously, allowing them more potency in affecting public consciousness that goes beyond the temporal and spatial limits of the play in the theatre, putting the playhouses in a position of adversarial debate with the authority of the state in ways that both draw attention to and undermine the supportive logic of how that state uses its power, not only through legislative and military force but also through the ideological life of the culture.[5] Such critics see Shakespeare as crucially questioning and subverting assumptions at the heart of his world concerning, for instance, the nature and place of women, of monarchical rule, of religion, and the nature of human life itself.

Though they differ in their conclusions, both approaches share certain assumptions. First, they do not doubt that the plays have political content and political consequences, though they disagree as to what those consequences are. They both see the plays not as the transhistorical work of a socially rootless genius, but as politically and contextually enmeshed. The plays are seen to explore complex issues of power at all possible levels, from that of the individual (where the power issues are typically rendered in terms of gender, race, and class) to that of the state and, where such readings push beyond the secular, into larger, more abstract concerns of status and autonomy even in matters spiritual. Where characters used to be considered as individuals who made certain choices and held personal beliefs, this more macro view tends to see the operation of larger social and economic forces which control the agency of those characters and define their values and assumptions.

Lady Macbeth, for instance, does not just manifest a crisis in identifying what it is to be female; she is constructed by it, her sense of self, her range of options, her notions of power and spousal identity, her obligations as a hostess, a wife, a mother (actual or speculative) are all shaped by the ways in which the world of the play defines gender, and her actions are balanced and contextualized by Lady Macduff, by the androgynous witches, and by the larger male dimension of the story, all of which inflect her identity. Notions of what it is to be masculine or feminine saturate the play, shape its characters, and propel its action. Feminist criticism has demonstrated the value of such a critical perspective on all the plays, scrutinizing their social environments in terms of the power dynamics, the range of agency open or denied to characters based on gendered expectations or assumptions—that sense of gendered identity as a construct to which the critics I referenced above championed. The predicament of Cordelia, the conflicting lure of Cleopatra, the gendered disguise to which so many of Shakespeare's comic heroines resort, all move around the fulcrum of gendered identity which, in the early modern context perhaps even more so than our own, is essentially political.

Similar arguments might be made about Othello's blackness, about Shylock's Jewishness, or about Caliban's status as slave in ways that approach the plays in terms of race, ethnicity, and an often postcolonialist sense of "Otherness." Indeed, it has become almost impossible in the post-slavery, post-holocaust, and post–civil rights era *not* to think about the plays in these terms as scholars and students continue (rightly, inevitably) to find contemporary resonance in these increasingly antique tales. Such approaches are a much needed counter to the Bardolotry of former ages which sought to efface ideas like race entirely as irrelevant or saw in the plays confirmation of damning stereotypes. We read *The Merchant of Venice* differently after the Holocaust because we must grapple with the idea that the play was, in some ways and regardless of how we might disagree with the reading—one of the constituent factors in the feeding of anti-Semitic fires which *produced* the Holocaust.

A study of *Romeo and Juliet* or *Henry IV Part I* might benefit from a shifting of focus from the titular characters to the various servants who populate the play, the social world of the story being thrown into sharp relief by a study of the power structures rooted in class. As Brecht was acutely aware, *Julius Caesar* and *Coriolanus* are plays whose political dimension shifts significantly when we look at the larger social world which the plays represent from the perspective of the poor, particularly if we can find analogues to Shakespeare's England in which riots over the price of basic foodstuffs and the stockpiling of grain in times of hardship had real and potentially destabilizing force. Of the great triumvirate of cultural studies (gender, race, and class), class is perhaps the least incendiary in the twenty-first century, but its rootedness in the plays, its centrality to their political dimension is as rich and undeniable in the literary classroom as it is for Brecht and Boal on stage.

Though they might be less shrill than the examples cited above, arguments could be centred on any character in Shakespeare which makes his or her individuality the product of (and in some ways less important than) that character's shaping socio-economic and cultural contexts. For such an approach, character is less like personhood and more like the imaginary discursive space which is produced out of material and ideological pressure. Reduced to its most extreme or vulgar form, characters become nexuses, points on the graph of social and economic conditions, driven less by will and agency then by the effect of those forces upon their current location in culture. Subtler and more insightful versions of this approach to the plays are so familiar and ubiquitous that I will spend no further time on them here except to say that for most literature students, the materialist and cultural studies perspectives which blossomed in the 1970s and 1980s, and their particular off shoot, identity politics, continue to define the ideas which are at work within or around Shakespeare's plays.

The second assumption shared by political readings of the plays, regardless of whether the critics concerned see them as bound to the ideology of the larger social order or assume that they manifest the subversive unravelling of that order, is that both groups of critics tend to root the plays in the culture which originally produced them. In other words, most political criticism of Shakespeare, regardless of its agenda, is historicist in assumption.

In the wake of New Historicism and Cultural Materialism, the notion that we must understand a period in order to understand the literature it produced has become a kind of scholarly truism. Since we have jettisoned both the transhistorical and the notion of literary production as the work of an individual author creating as if in a social vacuum, we must see literature as socially (and therefore historically) conditioned, shaped by its originating cultural moment, responding to (and in some ways—perhaps—fashioning) the debates and material conditions of its day, and ultimately confined to that period in terms of its range of meaning. The work of the scholar thus becomes the pursuit of an ever receding past in order to provide the necessary context by which we might understand plays which—though they may seem transparent and familiar—must finally be considered as the product of a historical Other. The past, as L.P. Hartley said, is a foreign country: they do things differently there (17).

I have been talking thus far about the plays as largely literary entities, but our concern here is the theatre, which, at least from the perspective of the literary critic or student, might also seem like a country almost as foreign as the past. The two worlds do communicate, of course, and it might be argued that political readings of the plays manifested themselves most aggressively through the work of theatre practitioners such as Jan Kott, Peter Brook, and Peter Hall before politics became central to literary study, but in certain respects the two spheres are separate and do not speak the same language. Even when both enact political readings, the form of those readings and the assumptions which underlie them are different and constructed by the terms of their respective cultures.

Let's take two of the core ideas of the literary approach and imagine them in the theatre, first, the idea that character is not individual but the nexus of various socially rooted forces and ideological pressures. On paper this works well enough, particularly in the classroom where a skilful teacher can leap from salient point to salient point within a character's speeches, focusing on those moments which build the larger case as one would if one was writing an argumentative essay. The theatre, however, does not work like this. Not everything Lady Macbeth says is clearly reducible to the gender issue, for instance, and while a teacher might simply ignore the rest as irrelevant to the trajectory of the class, a theatre production—and, more importantly, its audience—does not. The audience hears every line, more or less, regardless of how it serves a more schematic argument about larger social forces, and these affect the audience's sense of not only *what* Lady Macbeth is but also *who* she is. Because it is not simply a stray line passed over in the classroom as being itself unpolitical—say, "You lack the season of all natures, sleep" (3.5.142)—but everything about this Lady Macbeth on stage which insists upon a sense of individuality, of personhood, rather than merely the manifestation of social forces. Lady Macbeth is, after all, more than the sum of her lines, even if the actor assumes that the lines originate the part (which isn't necessarily the case). She is her stance, her gesture, her costume, her brand of attractiveness or sexual appeal, the way she moves, the tone of her voice, and a hundred other factors, none of them finally defined by the play as literary object, but all affecting how an audience reads her, all reinforcing the sense of her as a person, rather than as an idea. Theatre is concrete where literary discussion is necessarily abstract, and the physical presence of an actor embodying the part, giving utterance and life to the lines, reinforces a sense of depth, of three-dimensionality which is only reducable to abstraction with difficulty and by reading against the grain of the theatrical experience. This was, after all, one of Brecht's central concerns: that theatre—especially the bourgeois theatre, but maybe, finally and problematically, all theatre—unless the audience is somehow forcibly steered into seeing it in other ways, will always seem to show individuals making choices, rather than the larger social forces that manipulate them.

While we might discuss character in the literary classroom simply as the manifestation of scripted utterance which permits considerably greater abstraction in considering what that character is in terms of those large-scale social forces, character on stage is always the hybrid product of actor and role, and the result is a different kind of materiality which emphasizes the individual and the specific. It is not surprising therefore that character criticism, which reached its zenith in the glory days of Bardoltry before the advent of New Criticism and the formalism of the 1930s, though it has been reduced to a much-maligned footnote in literary study, lives on in the theatre. And while character criticism might be unselfconscious, sentimental, and reliant on dubious notions of Shakespeare's universal psychological applicability, it has a different order of importance and specificity in the theatre for both actors and audiences. Indeed, as Christy Desmet remarks, while character criticism has often served dominant ideologies and conservative political attitudes through claims that the plays reflect an absolute and unchanging view of humanity, "it need not do so" (Desmet *Character* 360). All but the most postmodern theatre produces plays as driven and manifested by characters who are—whatever else they are in larger social terms—individuals located in the bodies of the actors who personate them.

To return to the issue of identity politics, however, we might also ask—as critics such as Barbara Hodgdon and Sarah Werner do—what the presence of the expressly female body does in a contemporary production which complicates the play's meanings. Since theatrical meaning is built from performance and the conditions of production, not simply from the script, the presence of the actress in a part written for a boy player is a species of theatrically sanctioned intervention which resets the play's exploration of gender. Indeed, the body might be seen to overwrite the assumed literary meanings of the play, to create new ones with unanticipated but equally valid political valences. What those political valences are will depend on the specific production, its context, and its audience. As Werner says, "Placing the language of theatre alongside the language of Shakespeare, we discover that we are Shakespeare, not because he describes who we are, but because we describe our many selves in the process of staging his plays" (104).

This description of our "many selves," like Brecht's reference to the theatrical depiction of "men's lives together" makes the bridge from individual self to the politicized representation of identity. My point is not that identity politics in the mode of literary criticism loses its validity in the theatre—quite the contrary—but that the mode of signification radically alters the political semiotics of the moment, demanding that bodies, voices, gestures, and the other material stuff of the theatre become integral to how political meaning is made. Taking into account the entire performative apparatus of the theatre—particularly the presence of actual actors who stage gender, race, sexual orientation in their very presence—thus enables a new range of political possibilities which escape the apparent significations of the text alone and which, at least potentially, deconstruct the notion of Shakespeare as the Establishment voice of the dominant order. Thus Ayanna Thompson, who writes about African American Shakespeare performance, sees performance as permitting a range of productive options which exist between the old binaries of minorities being "freed by" or "freed from" Shakespeare (*Passing* 117). I return to critics who work with identity politics and Shakespeare in expressly theatrical terms in Chapter 3.

The second literary concern which strains under the pressure of theatrical performance is the assumption that analytical exploration of a play and its politics is necessarily a historically inflected endeavour. Any production of Shakespeare on stage has a historical dimension because the play (however adapted) is itself rooted in the past, and this knowledge colours the audience's reception of the show, but theatre is singularly grounded in the present, in the special dynamic of the live interaction of audience and performers, and so much of the history which roots literary study quickly becomes if not irrelevant then at least mediated and indirect. Productions cannot be thoroughly footnoted to explain lost historical contexts, and however meticulously one might be able to emulate the original playing conditions in terms of costumes, acting styles, and so on (always a vexed project) as at the reconstructed Globe theatre in London, one can never recreate the original theatrical dynamic because we cannot rebuild the original audience who were its co-creators. The foreignness of the past is essential to the historicist argument that we must embed ourselves in it as much as possible if we are to understand the plays, but theatre audiences cannot be thus trained, and theatre practitioners assume that the purpose of theatre is to communicate immediately and directly in the present, not to be engaged in a form of archaeological lecture about the play. However, we don't need to revert to old ideas about universalism and transhistoricism to assume that the plays can communicate in the present. Rather we must accept that the plays still communicate, but they communicate differently. We can make excellent literary arguments for the way that plays such as *Henry V* and *Richard II* respond to specifically Elizabethan concerns about power and those who wield it in ways containing various and potentially potent political resonances for their original audiences, but the specifics of those resonances are going to be largely lost on a contemporary audience, even if the programme peppers them with notes about how the crown came to be worn by Elizabeth's grandfather or the Essex rebellion of 1601. Some form of intellectual understanding might be achieved by such notes, but they cannot transform the manner of the play's semiotics so that they speak on a visceral level as they did to the crowds which watched them 400 years ago. However much a production might immerse itself in historical study during the research and rehearsal stages of the show, history is only obliquely relevant to the theatrical dynamic.

With these two points in mind—that most theatre foregrounds the individual rather than the macro-social and that history cannot be the root of a production's meanings—we must reimagine the political valences of theatrical Shakespeare without recourse to literary models. First, we must explore the extent to which such valences might be completely subsumed within the cultural myth of Shakespeare in ways which determine the political dimension of the plays in performance as part of a larger manifestation of the way elite culture replicates and evangelizes the values of the ruling social order. Whatever the political content of the plays—something which, as I have said, is always open to debate—Shakespeare has been utilized in culture for political ends based largely on assumptions about his literary quality, even about the innately apolitical content of his work, in ways designed to bolster a dominant social order. The social order has found—or claimed to find—in Shakespeare not so much proof of the rightness of its ideals as an abstract manifestation of them, and as such the teaching, staging, and export of Shakespeare might be seen as a form of evangelism on the part of white, British patriarchy in general, a notion of culture which values authority, which naturalizes power along the lines of class, race, gender, and ideology including religion. Such a view assumes that the very teaching of Shakespeare is an inculcation of a brand of culture into the lower social orders, the marginalized and the oppressed, which paradoxically reaffirms their status as inferior, as Other, or otherwise rightly disempowered. Such an idea is particularly central to the use of Shakespeare made by the Victorians in ways manifesting a species of English cultural supremacy (and a particular kind of Englishness at that) which was both a tool in and justification of the spread of the British Empire. As M. Keith Booker says of the British Raj:

> The invention of the tradition of English literature (with Shakespeare at its core) became a major tool of bourgeois hegemony in nineteenth-century Britain. At the same time, the incompleteness of British hegemony in India paradoxically made literature a crucial element of British power there.[6]

The principles which Shakespeare was assumed to enshrine were held to be universally applicable, but the application itself affirms a particular British cultural model which shows that universality—like God—speaks with an English accent. Other nations (cultures, classes, genders, non-normative sexualities, ideologies, etc.) are thus rendered lesser even by that which supposedly speaks to them of what it is to be human. Nor is such an idea merely the realm of the Victorians: identical assertions continue to abound to this day, most obviously in the work of popular scholars such as Harold Bloom whose applause for Shakespeare's universality contains a value judgement about what *ought to be* universal, though it is in fact the product of a particular cultural position (1–17). In other words, it is the very claim that Shakespeare is a model of all humanity and the pinnacle of artistic achievement, which allows it to be the tool of colonizers, oppressors and the elite. In appropriating Shakespeare to themselves, they insist upon an innate cultural superiority that denigrates whatever looks different. As Shakespeare is universal and thus defines what it is to be human, other artistic and cultural products can only express the specific, the lesser, the (logically speaking) subhuman. Confronted by such a monolith, all we can do—or so the argument goes—is embrace the values of the culture which brought such scripture to us, or labour on in knowing, damnable ignorance. This is the Shakespeare of the "Establishment": Shakespeare as (in Marjorie Garber's term) "fetish," that figure of nostalgia which, in its supposed universalizing, is most ideologically dangerous.[7]

Nor do we need look to Victorian colonization to see the hand of Establishment Shakespeare reaffirming hegemonic values. The late nineteenth century's institution of compulsory education in Britain and the United States provided a vehicle for the widespread study of Shakespeare as something self-evidently valuable, something which demanded the parallel invention of a new and potent wing of the Shakespeare industry, professionally trained expert teachers and scholars.[8] David Margolies observes that the nature of contemporary education and the need for students to be able to pass exams on Shakespeare which depend upon conventional wisdom deconstruct an individual response to the plays and forces instead an alienated and abstract sense of meaning which mystifies the plays, turning them into "pure cultural excellence" (43). Such a position insists upon the value of the plays while taking away from the student any sense of ownership, any means by which the nature of that value might be discovered for and by the individual reader, so that study of Shakespeare as a manifestation of larger cultural assumptions becomes an end in itself, and one which is designed to close off possible dissent.

As Graham Holderness says, it is the notion of Shakespeare as the mouthpiece of all that is elevated and valuable, all that is (particularly) Best of Britain, that is the root of the various and absurd arguments over who actually wrote the plays. The claim that only an aristocrat such as the Earl of Oxford could have written what was far too elevated for the mere son of a Stratford glove maker is evidence not just of snobbery (and a gross failure of the imagination) but of a sense of Shakespeare as rooted in and still growing from the heart of elite English culture (12). Such debates which seem biographical are thus revealed as intensely political, their historical dimension opening up beyond the particulars (frequently garbled) of the lives of the various contestants, to include 400 years of accreted cultural status and the corresponding and often insidious influence of an expressly political kind.

The theatre work of practitioners such as Boal, however, which I referred to in Chapter 1, affirms an essential localism to the political effects of performance which might be seen as trumping the larger cultural associations of a writer such as Shakespeare. Perhaps in spite of—and in some cases because of—the idea of Shakespeare as a tool of the hegemony, individual productions, or moments within productions might have quite different political resonances, particularly when we factor in (as per Knowles) the way that the political meanings of any production must be processed not just in terms of their scripts but in terms of their venues, the specific composition of their audiences, and so forth. Maybe the micro-specifics used in both textual analysis and historical research, detail-oriented arguments which have so fuelled the rethinking of the plays' politics in the literary field, might be applied to performance in related ways, so that we escape Shakespeare's monolithic status in culture by focusing on a particular Hamlet's playing of a particular moment, in a particular performance space, for an equally particular audience. If it is possible that such specifics might generate altogether different political energies from those generally afforded an Establishment Shakespeare, then that very "Establishment" status gives the plays an aura of venerable respectability which functions as a stalking horse from which a production might shoot less orthodox ideas and impulses. Simply put, not only is staged Shakespeare not necessarily limited to hegemonic conservatism, it may well be used as a kind of Trojan horse, which might potentially undermine that hegemony from the inside.

Even if we concede such a point, however, it is undeniable that the case of a political staged Shakespeare is a tricky one, one over which 400 years of accumulated cultural history looms. As Knowles affirms the particularity of place in assessing theatrical meaning, affecting as it does the mindset of the (plural) audience, we must also acknowledge that the aegis of Shakespeare in and of itself affects that mindset too. Yet identifying the precise form of the effect on that (again, plural) audience takes us out of large-scale abstraction and into the kinds of specifics which are extremely difficult to track. There is no question, for instance, that Shakespeare's name attracts audiences who would not come to see plays by Middleton, Jonson, or Decker because of a sense of value inferred from education and culture at large, the theatrical experience somehow validating the audience's sense of their elite status and, in the process, reifying certain conservative values. But there is also no question that Shakespeare's name will repel many possible audience members whose theatrical tastes run more, for instance, to musicals or contemporary comedy. Some audience members will come to Shakespeare unwillingly to get their culture shot or because teachers, friends, or romantic partners drag them along. For such audiences, Shakespeare's Establishment status is, simply put, a turn-off, something fusty, irrelevant, and tedious, something hard to understand and finally belonging to social groups from which the audience feels, for good or ill, separated. Such audience members take their seats prepared to be bored or irritated, poised, perhaps, to reject whatever ideology the play offers, and while it might be argued that Establishment Shakespeare works insidiously, acting on the audience from within its aura of respectability, I'm far from sure that contemporary audiences are so quick to accept such an aura.

Establishment Shakespeare is, as has already been argued, a condition of modernity which originates in the nineteenth century. The postmodern condition which so saturates the twenty-first century puts special strain on the very idea of authority, particularly as a cultural force for hegemony, so that it seems retrograde, contrary to the particular brand of individualism which so shapes contemporary identity and its attendant attitudes. Many regional Shakespeare festivals in the United States, for instance, seem to struggle more and more to find younger audiences, something which is as much a *result* of Shakespeare's place in education as it is in spite of it. In Britain and the United States, audiences for Shakespeare tend to be bifurcated: young audiences of students brought by their schools to matinee productions on the one hand and, on the other, considerably older audiences in the evening shows. This latter group, with a few exceptions, is (in contrast to those school groups) predominantly white, well educated, affluent, and—by virtue of age— less driven by the spirit of postmodernity in art, politics, and sense of self.

This demographic fact puts theatre companies under particular pressures as those evening audiences die off—metaphorically speaking in hard economic times, but also literally. Too few of those student audiences grow up to become theatregoers to take the place of the increasingly elderly audiences for whom Establishment Shakespeare is still part of the draw. The double-bind is a real one. Companies are wary of edgier approaches to Shakespeare which might alienate their current clientele, but know that old fashioned productions which reinforce high school prejudices will cut their collective throats in the future. These are commercial concerns rather than artistic ones, perhaps, but both participate in the generation of a theatre's political dimension and must be taken seriously.

So how can staged Shakespeare, burdened as it is with its own cultural weight and appealing most readily to those least likely to want that cultural weight problematized by political subversion, find a voice which does something other than reaffirm its own hegemonic status? How can Shakespeare in the theatre be consciously and counter-culturally political? This book assumes that it can be, indeed that it must be, but it also assumes that the staging of a political Shakespeare is a complex business built on details, on specifics which go well beyond a critical approach to the text itself. It also assumes that, try as it might, any given production will run into insurmountable obstacles. Some people who might be open to its political approach simply will not come to the theatre, partly because Shakespeare's Establishment status will keep them away. Others who go to the show in part *because* of that Establishment status will be impervious to any attempts to deconstruct, subvert, or question the values of that Establishment, so rooted is their conviction about what Shakespeare is.

Such a phenomenon speaks to what we have already discussed with regard to Shakespeare's curious dual status as literary artefact on the one hand and theatrical entertainment on the other. Problematically, the cultural power of Shakespeare is more dependent on the former than the latter, partly because text is (or rather is perceived to be) fixed and stable in ways that theatre is not, but more generally because it is in its literary form that Shakespeare's heritage has enjoyed the greatest power in the school room and as the quotable font of wisdom and beauty in culture more generally. The result is that the text is often assumed to trump the production where the two are perceived to be in opposition, thereby allowing sceptical audiences to fall back on preconceived notions of what a text says to counter (and vanquish) what a production might do if it violates their sense of political decorum.

I have written before about a moment in a production of *Twelfth Night* in Georgia in which Viola, disguised as the boy Cesario, and Orsino, caught up in an intimate and touching moment kissed briefly before Viola's true gender had been revealed. The production was attesting to a relationship which would flower at the end of the play when Viola, her femininity confessed, could marry Orsino. The point of the production (and, I would argue, the play) was that love was not gender-dependent though marriage (within the world of the play and the author) was. What the audience saw, of course, was an apparent homosexual encounter which, for some, was not mitigated by the fact that the actor playing Viola was, in fact, female. Orsino thought her male, so the kiss was "gay." I witnessed one indignant audience member triumphantly returning to her friends after an intermission trip to the gift shop where she was able to confirm that the kiss "wasn't in the book!"

The implication was clear. The production was in violation of the text, and its authority as a vehicle for Shakespeare (with his attendant Establishment status as property of and advocate for right-thinking heterosexuals) had collapsed. It didn't matter to this audience member that the kiss was not prohibited by the text, any more than the text prohibited the fact that this Orsino was reclining on a cushion or that the music which accompanied the scene was played on a cello. The text was seen as the locus and origin of all meaning, so the production's decision to add the semiotically potent kiss was a directorial interpolation of the worst and most adaptive kind which changed the play and, in the process, stripped the production of Shakespeare's authorizing power.

Of course, many arguments can be made against such a response. All theatrical production is adaptation, the genre of the book being transformed to the systems of signification of the stage in which the script itself is merely one of many necessary creators of meaning. The audience member in question had nothing negative to say about the costuming, the light or the music, all of which were extra-textual, so the grounds of her complaint are exposed as a conventional ruse; her objection to the kiss was that she didn't like the idea of it, didn't like what it said about love or about Shakespeare. In short, for her the production ran into an ideological impasse. The psychological rightness of the moment which I felt, its beauty and the way it prepared for an ending which was more than mere convenience, was unable to alter her preconceptions or what I'm sure she thought of as her values.

Such, I'm afraid, is life in the theatre. There is only so much you can do in leading this particular horse to water. If it won't drink, it won't drink. The problem with the example above, of course, is that the horse that won't drink may also deny that what you have offered is actually water at all. "It's not in the book," means "it's not really Shakespeare." It might look like it, even sound like it, but where it deviates from the audience's assumptions about what they are going to see, there is always the danger that it will finally be dismissed as mere adaptation, driven less by the play than by the supposed trendy or radical agenda of puppeteers who insist on jerking Shakespeare's strings rather than letting him speak for himself in the voice the audience are accustomed to.

Political productions of Shakespeare (and here I am talking of conventional stagings of the plays in commercial theatres, rather than—say—radically adaptive guerrilla theatre happenings in public spaces) walk a fine line which is drawn by the playwright's cultural appeal. That which attracts many audience members, the experience they think they are coming to see, must be used and then subverted but in such a way that the audience are taken with the production, so that their sense is of the show enacting a new, radical but valid version of Shakespeare. Of course, different audiences may be guided in different ways, and for some a jettisoning of Shakespearean authority along the way might be welcome and exciting in ways that does not undermine the credibility of the production. For many, however, leaving the theatre with a sense that what they experienced somehow wasn't Shakespeare at all, risks (though it does not necessarily effect) the rejection of the production's political thrust. The paradox of Shakespeare's appeal to some audiences is that their desire to see Him in all his God-like wisdom is an end in itself, not a means to other thoughts or feelings, and for such audiences, political ideas have to be explored with care and, usually, subtlety. Audiences who come in with fewer assumptions are likely to be more open to radical productions, but such audiences are, by the same logic, harder to attract in the first place. Of course, pleasing conservative audiences so that they will keep coming back is no justification for any kind of production, and I would argue that if doing Shakespeare that feels exciting, contemporary and politically interesting will drive away some audiences, it's best to let them go. Getting an audience to come to and sit through a Shakespeare production you privately think is politically retrograde or pandering to the worst assumptions about what Shakespeare should be is no achievement at all.

Whether or not Shakespeare's Establishment associations draw or repel audiences may come down to questions of ownership. Whose Shakespeare is this which is being staged? One of the impulses in recent theatrical Shakespeare, motivated—at least in part—by the aforementioned dwindling and elderly audiences and fuelled by various educational impulses, sometimes with significant state backing, might be called the democratizing of Shakespeare. Rather than being the domain of a cultural elite, Shakespeare is, as The Shakespeare Theatre in Washington DC used to put it, "for all!" What this means, of course, is open to debate. Are we merely shaking the cultural superflux to the poor naked wretches in our schools and streets so that we ensure the continued survival of the theatre and the Shakespeare industry while inculcating those less socially privileged with the values of the ruling elite which reinforce a sense of the naturalness of the status quo? Or are we truly granting ownership of Shakespeare to those marginalized and disadvantaged so that the plays will be made to—or allowed to—speak of their concerns and ideas with their voices?

Answering such questions requires close analysis of production specifics, but a sense of the general issues might be gathered through one instance of the so-called democratizing of Shakespeare: racial cross-casting. The argument is a familiar one. Actors of colour have traditionally been limited to a handful of roles in which their race may be a useful signifier: Othello, for instance, or Aaron the Moor in *Titus Andronicus*. More recently, casts of Shakespeare plays have become more diverse, though the logic for such casting varies from company to company and show to show. Some utilize what they term "colour-blind" casting, in which the actor's race is irrelevant to the part he or she plays, ignored by everyone on stage and, supposedly, the audience as well. Such an approach might cast Lear's three daughters without a consistent racial "look," a white Goneril, say, with a black Cordelia and a Latina Regan. The democratizing impulse is to allow actors of colour to play parts they would otherwise not be able to perform, allowing them to "own" Shakespeare in ways formerly denied to them, and in the process, their race or ethnicity is assumed to be effaced by the production. Critics of such an approach object that race vanishes on stage no more than it does in life outside the theatre and that failure to acknowledge it creates logical problems within the play (as Lear's multiracial family flies in the face of biology if we are not to assume that the king had multiple wives of different racial origins). More problematic is the idea that such an approach is actually a denial of race as a signifying factor, an obfuscation of something which is actually crucial to the actor's identity. From such a perspective, "colour-blind" casting becomes a form of cultural colonialism, in which the non-white person is patronizingly inducted into the Western literary, theatrical, and cultural canon, their race scrubbed out in the process of becoming "universal."[9] Some actors of colour take the objection further, refusing to play parts like Othello which, they argue, were written by a white author for a white actor and a white audience and which play upon and further racial stereotypes. Such critics do not want to own Shakespeare or to condone the idea that he owns them and argue that this is a place for "blackface" casting, so that race in the production is underlined as conspicuously and problematically fictive.[10]

Conversely, non-traditional racial casting might be used in plays whose focus is less clearly about race, and in ways consistent with the internal logic of the play. A production of *Romeo and Juliet*, for instance, which defines the Capulets and Montagues along racial lines or sidesteps the idea of race as the source of the division by casting both families with black actors, may facilitate a different brand of ownership, though doing so will necessitate a grappling with the casual Elizabethan racism which underscores the equation of ugliness with blackness as when Juliet is compared to "a rich jewel in an Ethiop's ear."

In terms of the identity politics with which I begun this chapter and which undergirds the next, it seems clear that a version of Shakespeare (the "Bard" of the Victorian tradition) is or was elitist and exclusionary, the Establishment figure understandably loathed by all who felt alienated from his version of normative culture. But theatrical meaning lies in its performed specifics, its material environment, the bodies of its players, all of which must be weighed in order to assess the production's political meanings, and a new wave of politically inflected Shakespeareans are now doing precisely this. For these critics, the political valences of Shakespeare on stage cannot be read simply from text, from history or from broad-based cultural or educational associations with the plays' author, lying rather in the details of the individual production. Lizbeth Goodman, for instance, cites a range of alternative

Shakespeares which celebrate the work of women in the theatre, some of which are radical new plays created in response to Shakespeare, others which rethink Shakespeare in ways which refuse to allow old ideas to marginalize or dominate the women involved in them.[11] She offers, for instance, a close reading of Fiona Shaw playing Rosalind in Tim Alberry's 1989 *As You Like It*, in which the actress's ownership of the role subverted elements of the romantic plot as traditionally imagined and conveyed a sense of power and autonomy through her body language, gesture, and the ease with which she cross-dressed as Ganymede. Shaw affirmed that her hold on the part was not the result of foregrounding gender but of focusing instead on theatrical components such as rhythm, presentation, and power, refusing to be cowed by the idea that the part might be said to diminish her as a woman. The result, according to Goodman, was a display of ease and potency which redrew the power dynamics of the play and made her the dominant party:

> The process of creating alternatives as enacted by Shaw is built upon a recognition of a working dynamic between gender and power, which informs her characterization of both male and female parts, and which is stressed in performance, where acting (in practice) takes priority over the (feminist) theory of performance. Shaw's presentation of androgyny contributes to a greater act of subversion that takes into account her personal context and ambivalence about elements of the British tradition, and thereby liberates her, as a performer, to create alternatives that are authentic both to the requirements of Shakespeare and to herself. (212)

Ayanna Thompson is following a similar impulse when she advocates that we "leave Shakespeare behind" in matters of race and performance, not in the sense of ceasing to read, study, or stage the plays, but by sloughing off "the cultural force of Bardolatry" ("Blackface Bard"). Only by escaping the fantasy of the author's intentionality can black practitioners redefine what Shakespeare on stage is, and that requires a sense of ownership on behalf of those practitioners that somehow overwrites the cultural assumptions audiences may bring with them. This is no easy task, but it is attainable over time and in the specifics of individual productions.

Recent application of queer theory to Shakespeare on stage has found much to interrogate and celebrate, some of which grows out of reimagining the original (all male) playing conditions, out of cross-dressing or out of other elements of plays such as *Twelfth Night* whose staging, as critics such as Chad Allen Thomas have pointed out, permits—even invites—an exploration of homoerotics or other non-heterosexual identity.[12]

Ownership of Shakespeare, it seems, necessitates a degree of refashioning, particularly if a production is to be more than a critical commentary on the play's problematic origins or legacy. This raises questions about the purpose of claiming something which has to be tailored so as not to be itself offensive, but such a process assumes—rightly, to my mind—that there is value to what is being claimed which survives the adaptive strategy. Democratizing Shakespeare, then, if it is to be more than cultural evangelism in the service of the Establishment, must rethink what Shakespeare is as well as who it is for, and in this project identity politics is especially useful. Indeed, all production must embrace Shakespeare not as a thing to be offered up to its audience, but as a potential which is given form not by any kind of prior absolute or ontological presence but by the expressly theatrical energies which will shape its meaning. In this, the material conditions of theatre must be permitted to trump both literary readings and the larger cultural associations of the play and the position held by its increasingly abstracted author. In Bennett's terms, the theatre which brings Shakespeare to life on stage is both transitive and intransitive, the staging of a prior object (the script) and the creation of something entirely new. Theatrical meaning does not reside within Shakespeare's words, nor can an allegiance to those words govern theatrical purpose, particularly if that purpose is to have a political dimension. The theatre is an interpretive and constructive response to those words, not simply a transmission of them, so that the political production must wrestle not with what a play means but what it *might* mean, what it *might be made* to mean as its literary and historical dimension encounters the contemporary and immediate collaborative forces of company members and audiences some of whose interests, whose very selves, have been excluded from Shakespeare on stage for centuries. In such a way, the play meets the specific needs of the present. From this vital chemistry will the production emerge, and the constructive process necessarily changes all the original and originary elements. Only if we can embrace such an idea, can we talk meaningfully about democratizing a theatrical Shakespeare.

Part II
In Practice

3
Identity Politics and the Stage

The three plays I will consider in this chapter—*Othello*, *The Merchant of Venice*, and *The Taming of the Shrew*—have all been considered so politically incendiary in their representation of race, ethnicity, and gender that some theatre practitioners now refuse to stage them at all. Each play represents, it is argued, a normative early modern perspective which has played a part in the perpetuation of stereotypes, disempowerment, and injustice in ways which have had real and damaging consequences for the world outside the theatre both for individuals and for society as a whole. One of them, *The Merchant of Venice*, might even be called a contributor to the culture which produced a genocide. Even if we can escape the plays' historical associations, some say they contain ideas and assumptions which are offensive. As such they have no place on the contemporary stage and—regardless of their other laudable qualities—should be consigned to the trash bin of history.

These are expressly theatrical arguments in that an audience is drawn into the story of a play in performance—as Brecht knew—in ways that disable some of the critical distance possible when one simply reads it. While we might contextualize the plays historically in the classroom, explaining how they manifest the assumptions of their period and thinking through the consequences of such assumptions, the theatre draws us into the logic of the plays, subjects us to the visceral power of spectacle, character association, and the affecting potency of human action played out in front of our eyes in ways which feel immediate and contemporary. In her extended discussion of the politics of the *Taming of the Shrew* on stage, Sarah Werner has this to say:

> Katherine, no matter what the history of enclosure or theories of subjectivity reveal, has a personal story to tell on stage. It is in her

story that [Barbara] Hodgdon locates the play's subversive pleasure, the excitement of constituting her character the way we want to. But it is also in her story that the play's danger lies, the risk that audiences will read it in a way that validates their own potentially patriarchal desires. (77)

Werner goes on to analyse the 1995 Royal Shakespeare Company (RSC) production of the play directed by Gale Edwards, drawing particular attention to the frequency with which female directors at the RSC (still a comparatively rare breed) are saddled with responsibility for this troubling play, as if being expected to save it or legitimize it by virtue of their gender alone. This particular production, Werner says, used the framing induction centred on Christopher Sly to foreground the whole as a patriarchal fantasy, the "success" of which left its Petruchio—who was confronted by the enormity of what he had done to the woman he had "tamed"—humbled and apologetic. Newspaper critics hated it, the right-leaning papers lamenting the emasculating feminist influence of the director, while the left decried the exposure of the play's bullying misogyny without somehow solving it so that several critics ended with thoughts that the play should be abandoned as too out of step with current social politics to merit staging.[1]

Ayanna Thompson cites Dympna Callaghan's remark that "Othello was a white man"—that is that the part was written to be played by a white actor, by a white author, for a white audience—in her approach to discussing the casting of the play (*Passing Strange* 97). She goes on to cite instances of critics making the case that Othello should not be played by a black actor on the contemporary stage, one potent case for which is articulated by black British actor Hugh Quarshie:

> If a black actor plays Othello does he not risk making racial stereotypes seem legitimate and even true?...Of all parts of the canon, perhaps Othello is the one which should most definitely not be played by a black actor. (99)

One alternative is to return to the early modern staging convention of blackface, though this is similarly fraught with problems. Using a range of non-Shakespearean examples, Thompson scrutinizes not only instances when the supposedly satirical use of blackface seems to grow out of actual racism but also cases where audience response—which is always beyond the control of the director or performer—may (wilfully?) misread what is being staged.[2] Such performances may unintentionally bolster racist ideas in the audience, and while this is a common problem outside Shakespeare, Thompson locates *Othello* as its troubling origin point:

> This fear [of unintentionally reinforcing racist stereotypes] is familiar and has been explored in many plays, novels, films, and, of course, literary and performance criticism. In fact, one might even label it the "Othello syndrome" because *Othello* is one of the first Western texts to demonstrate the potential violent outcome of internalizing the racist constructions of blackness. (105–106)

Similar problems dominate *The Merchant of Venice* which gives us a selection of potentially racist stereotypes in Arragon, Morocco, and Shylock, the last of which is doubly loaded on the contemporary stage by the historical weight of the twentieth century. As Harold Bloom says, "the Holocaust made and makes 'The Merchant of Venice' unplayable, at least in what appear to be its own terms" (Brantley). Cary Mazer writes about his own ambivalence towards serving as dramaturg for a Pennsylvania production of the play (a job, he says, he got not only because he was a Shakespeare scholar, an expert on the play's performance history, but also—even primarily—because he was a Jew), saying that however Shakespeare humanizes Shylock, the anti-Semitic stereotypes remain clearly visible within the play and not just in the epithets hurled by the problematic Christians:

> It is no wonder, then, that for all of the productions over the past century that were sympathetic to Shylock (and for all of the Jewish actors who played the role, such as David Warfield, Morris Carnovsky, Albert Basserman, David Suchet, Dustin Hoffman, Antony Sher, Ron Liebman, Henry Goodman, and others) the play has been strangely attractive to anti-Semites. Werner Krauss, who had played Shylock in one of the many pre-WWII German productions directed by Max Reinhardt, reprised the role for a blatantly anti-Semitic production in Germany sponsored by the Nazis, capitalizing on his notoriety for playing the villainous title character in the notorious propaganda movie, *Jew Süss*. And even productions with a far less sinister agenda have—intentionally or inadvertently—played into the play's seductive anti-Semitism. When the reconstruction of the original Globe Theatre finally opened in London for its first season in 1997, the Artistic Director discovered that the audience at their premiere production of *Henry V* enjoyed booing the French generals standing in

the way of Henry's victorious conquest of France; wishing to reprise this sense of audience involvement, they revived *The Merchant of Venice* the next year, inviting the audience to boo at Shylock, to laugh at his agonies over his daughter's betrayal, and to cheer when he is finally ignominiously banished from the stage. I'm glad I wasn't there to see it.

And so, I sometimes wish the play would just go away.[3]

The stories of these plays present, it is argued, some of the most appalling and persistent ideas of western hegemonic culture: that non-white people, however "civilized" by their presence in European culture, are credulous savages, and that interracial marriage is an abomination with necessarily tragic consequences; that Jews are merciless, money-hungry, and cruel, their danger mitigated only by a lack of higher intellect, and that the natural way of dealing with them is to strip them of land, property, and religion; that women's natural place is to be demure, passive, and obedient to fathers and husbands and that if they persist in being otherwise they should be beaten into submission.

Pretty damning stuff.

That there are opposing views of these plays that can be argued through close textual analysis doesn't counter the problem of how the theatre might subvert the more retrograde position without recourse to literary gloss, historical footnote, and so forth. Most importantly, their acceptability cannot rely on their status as simply Shakespeare, whose greatness and perspicacity might be seen as endorsing for the present the horrors and absurdities of the past.

Though black actors such as Ira Aldridge and Paul Robeson played Othello (in 1825 and 1930, respectively), the tradition of casting a white man in the role persisted well into the 1970s (Olivier played the part on film in 1965). Though the practice has been largely abandoned, some African American actors—as I have already said—have used versions of Jonathan Miller's defence of casting Anthony Hopkins in the title role for the BBC television production in 1981: having Othello played by a black actor might encourage the audience to "equate the supposed simplicity of the black with the exorbitant jealousy of the character" (Potter 154). Yet Miller's attempt to sidestep the issue of race paradoxically left him open to charges of racism for denying the role to an actor of colour, despite the fact that he originally offered the part to James Earl Jones, only to have the deal blocked by Actor's Equity. In spite of the argument that *Othello* was written by a white playwright for a white actor and an audience which had minimal first-hand experience of black people, most companies seem to assume that Othello should be played by an actor of colour, if only to sidestep the historically loaded associations of blackface. The nagging anxiety which dogs many modern productions, therefore, is that in manifesting a credulous and ultimately murderous black man, the play enacts the familiar and inherently racist notion of the "noble savage."

Productions often counter this approach by attempting to render Othello in psychologically specific terms, as an individual rather than the representation of his entire race, though this is difficult when he is the only black man on stage. As in productions of *The Merchant of Venice*, a kind of solution might be found in embracing this sense of separateness and alienation, but Shylock's and Othello's cases are different. The former has been demonized and mistreated by the Christian majority all his life, and it is not difficult to imagine—even to sympathize with—his thirst for revenge on the man who most stands for the Christian business community. Othello, by contrast has been revered by the Venetians. If he is a victim of racism, its tendrils are subtler, more difficult to spot, until Iago starts to exploit the cultural anxieties concerning interracial marriage and a mistrust of the Moor held even by those who seemed to honour him, such as Desdemona's father, Brabantio. A textual study can easily point up the way Iago exploits Othello's latent discomfort with not being Venetian born in feeding him misogynistic "insight" into the nature of Venetian women and pressing ideas about the unnaturalness of Desdemona's appetites in choosing Othello in the first place.

But the stage, as I have already said, does not necessarily lend itself to nuanced literary argument, particularly when the subtleties of the arcane text are set against the potent, post–civil rights era visuals of a black actor murdering his white wife in a fit of jealous rage premised on the slenderest of evidence. In 1997, the Shakespeare Theatre in Washington DC sought to foreground the race issue with what they called a photonegative production: a white actor (Patrick Stewart) playing Othello, surrounded by a largely black cast. The language of race in the script was left unaltered, so one might expect that what the audience saw was a pointedly ironic commentary on the play's racial dynamics, forcing the audience to understand Othello's marginal position through the jarring inversion which made the white man a minority even within that bastion of western culture, Shakespeare, and that oft-invoked model of racial prejudice, *Othello*. The timing of the production was also significant because less than two years earlier one of the most famous legal battles and attendant media circuses in recent history had occurred: the trial of African American former running back O.J. Simpson for the murder of his Caucasian wife, Nicole. The case often divided the country along racial lines and it inevitably ghosted traditionally cast productions of Othello (i.e. shows with black Othellos and white Desdemonas). Perhaps this production would escape the knee-jerk racism many felt that the Simpson case had highlighted. Stewart was an acclaimed Shakespearean whose days at the RSC predated his recent work for film and television, but that work would surely loom large in attracting an audience. He was, after all, not just an actor but a celebrity currently riding the massive high of *Star Trek: the Next Generation* which had ended on television three years earlier and had transferred to the big screen with *Generations* (1995) and *First Contact* (1996).

Much about the production was praised, but as a rethinking of the play's racial politics it was largely deemed a failure and for interesting reasons which bolster some of the arguments I have already made about how meaning in theatre is created. First, part of the initial rationale was problematized by the nature of the audience. As Lois Potter points out, some of the impulse to stage the photonegative production in the first place came from the fact that Washington DC has a very large African American population, much of it in the vicinity of the theatre, but comparatively under privileged. Yet this population was not represented extensively in the audience demographics, which tended to be dominated by the other populations of the city: politicos and tourists. In America, Stewart's following is predominately white, partly because African Americans comprise a comparatively small portion of the sci-fi fan base, and this—coupled with the general difficulty experienced at American theatres of drawing minority audiences to Shakespeare—probably accounts for the audience demographic issues at least as much as ticket prices which, at $15.00–$50.00 per person, could not be considered unreasonable even by 1997 standards.[4]

The critical response to the show was almost unanimous in its sense that Stewart completely dominated the production, in part because of his superior skill as a player of Shakespeare and partly because of his fame. It is difficult to track how celebrity plays on stage, but it seems undeniable that a sizeable portion of a theatre audience (whose attendance is more deliberate and expensive than those catching a movie or chancing on a TV show at home) are there in part because of the star's prior credits. Many will be fans, predisposed to see that star outshine his fellow cast members. This is not to fault Stewart's intent or performance, but it is a condition of the semiotics of theatre and celebrity culture. Couple that with his Englishness, his specifically

British training and attendant facility with the Shakespearean text, and the problem becomes not only aesthetic but also political, albeit unintended, even opposed to the original purpose of the production. A largely white audience left the theatre with their assumptions confirmed: Shakespeare—even at his most racially charged and in a production designed to push that charge to the uttermost—is best played by a white Englishman.

The apparent failure of the production's political thrust indicates a problem with the way in which such a bold casting choice inevitably makes the play about race, presenting as it does a persistent visual which serves as commentary on, even critique of, the play, but tends to reduce it to a single idea. When the star power of the lead, the nature of the audience and other concerns conspire to derail that idea, the production seems to get lost in its own conceit. Stagings which take a more realist approach to casting face different problems in their presentation of the idea of race, but their range of meanings is potentially broader and more subtle. Moreover, they allow the production to be about more than simply race. For Trevor Nunn in 1989, for instance, the play was about a military culture and, by extension, the difficult place of women within it (Potter 188–192), an approach which personalized and nuanced the politics of the play while sacrificing a broader statement. Other productions have defused or complicated the play's racial politics by casting actors of colour in other roles. Bianca is frequently non-Caucasian, and some productions have added black servants or populated the Cypress scenes with non-white actors. Some shows (Charles Marrowitz's 1972 adaptation is one) have even used non-white Iagos, a choice which problematizes his participation in racist discourse (assuming those lines are kept), but which does not necessarily render them nonsensical, making him rather an Uncle Tom, a version of the colonized who desperately, and in ways marked by self-loathing and cultural betrayal, tries to mimic the values of the dominant culture. Such an approach might be subtle and psychologized, but it is no less political for that.

The photonegative production in Washington DC might be called Brechtian in its ambition, relying as it did on a distancing effect, particularly the disjunction of the racial visuals from the language of the text, the play becoming less a realist window on character and action as in Nunn than a scrutiny of the play's position in racial history and relations. But the "alienation" existed only in the photonegative and not in other Brechtian effects which might have foregrounded the political agenda (non-realist acting, for instance), so its point was subsumed within a production which was read and evaluated in largely realist terms in spite of the casting. The bold stroke was not, apparently, bold enough to drive the political point home, and the critical response—premised as it was on supposedly apolitical concerns—proved positively subversive to that point. One can't help wondering how the show's political valences would have been read without a star like Stewart in the role or with a more radical notion of performance undergirding the whole.

The difficulty of navigating broad-strokes political productions through non-traditional casting applies to gender as well as race. In 2003, the reconstructed Globe Theatre in London reversed the original staging practice by producing *The Taming of the Shrew* with an all female cast, starring Janet McTeer as Petruchio and Kathryn Hunter as Kate. An interpolated prologue punningly announced the show as "redressing the balance" of single-sex production, an act which is itself a political statement, a reclaiming of this most vexed of plays from its patriarchal origins. McTeer's Petruchio was impressive—a tall, swaggering, womanizing cartoon of masculinity—while Hunter's Kate was diminutive, unconventional as a romantic lead, occasionally sympathetic in the hardships she had to endure and finally unbreakable. In her notorious final speech in which she manifests the extent of how her feistiness has been tamed into gendered humility and obedience which she says should be modelled by the other wives, Hunter made real to me a familiar feminist reading of the play which I had always thought strained: she still has her voice and can speak at length in ways contradicting the broken humility of the speech's content. In performance, Hunter gave the first part of the speech demurely, gently reprimanding Bianca and the widow for their behaviour:

> Fie, fie! unknit that threatening unkind brow,
> And dart not scornful glances from those eyes,
> To wound thy lord, thy king, thy governor...
> Thy husband is thy lord, thy life, thy keeper,
> Thy head, thy sovereign; one that cares for thee,
> And for thy maintenance commits his body
> To painful labour both by sea and land,
> To watch the night in storms, the day in cold,
> Whilst thou liest warm at home, secure and safe;
> And craves no other tribute at thy hands
> But love, fair looks and true obedience;
> Too little payment for so great a debt.
>
> (5.2.140–158)

At this point she paused, apparently done, whereupon the "men" on stage began complementing Petruchio on his victory, only to be interrupted by Kate starting up again, the rest of the speech becoming steadily more ironic, more mocking, till—dancing out of Petruchio's reach—she jumped up onto the table and brayed the rest of the speech about women's natural subservience, showing off her legs before a mortified Petruchio. The female characters laughed riotously and the men were abashed and humiliated by this puncturing of their triumph, while Kate stormed off, leaving Petruchio hanging pointedly after his "Come on and kiss me, Kate."[5]

It was a glorious moment: funny and potent, and one which utterly destabilized the play's gendered conclusion without recourse to the subtle psychological negotiation which actors usually rely upon these days to render Kate's final speech a kind of private joke between her and Petruchio, a joke which is premised on the idea that the play is finally a romantic comedy in which the fractious couple have found common ground (usually in the sun/moon scene of act IV scene V). Yet I couldn't help wonder if the cross-casting helped or hindered the production's final political point. Re-dressing the balance is all well and good, but did we need a female actor, however wonderful, as Petruchio to make the ending work? Rather, did not the theatrical effect of the cross-dressing rather mitigate against the power of that ending by rendering the gendering issue a bit of a pantomime gag. Several reviewers wrote disparagingly of the supporting cast's fake masculinity, reducing the production to the level of the slightly embarrassing efforts of an all girls school. Such dismissal (though it was never aimed at McTeer's Petruchio which was largely accepted as both compelling and amusing) may smack of latent misogyny, but it also comes from the same reluctance to accept the kind of Brechtian halfway house which we saw in the photonegative *Othello*: the show was and was not realist, the actors were and were not intended to be visible within their roles, and the point of the cross-dressing consequently became both muddy and ignorable as an irrelevance. Though accepting the regendering as a convention rooted vaguely in the authorizing past of the original Globe, audiences and critics were not then invited to think unduly about it, and the final political jab—effective though it was—grew less from the casting convention or an obvious discourse on gender as social construct or theatrical guise, as it did out of normative psychology: Kate refused to be tamed, and though her performance might be seen as reading against the grain of what her speech actually said, it made perfect sense within an essentially realist reading of the production. That there were women playing men in the show finally didn't seem any more important than the fact that one of the women also played Petruchio's spaniel, Troilus.

The regendered Globe *Shrew* may not have foregrounded the constructed nature of gender itself, but it did remind the audience that the play was written from a distinctly male perspective which had now been reversed. It was a partisan production which suggested that the play was too. The ending's refusal to solve the final tension was a perfectly credible way of integrating a wryly gendered defiance into the internal logic of the play so that the production was a "legitimate" manifestation of the script and not simply a critical response to it. An extra political dimension—and one which ghosts all questions of non-traditional casting—is thus revealed: the question of ownership. Since roles for women and people of colour have been traditionally limited in Shakespeare (in accord with the plays as written and the culture from which they emerged), there is an understandable impulse to want to open them up to new ways of casting which create more opportunities for actors. Two questions result from such non-traditional casting. The first is one which dogs this entire study: is the very impulse to non-traditional casting a kind of colonialism in which non-white male performers are inducted into a fundamentally bardolotrous position by being granted roles to which they must subsume their true natures? Though gender-"blind" casting, like colour-blind casting, seems to me neither possible nor desirable, I can imagine no meaningful objection to casting where race or gender are assumed to stay visible on stage, nor do I see such casting as innately bardolotrous, since it is dependent on the particularities of the production.

The second question is whether ownership by actresses and people of colour radiates beyond the playing space and stands in for ownership on the part of corresponding elements of the audience. This is harder to assess and should be gauged on a case-by-case basis, by which I mean not just show by show but audience member by audience member. Such data may be largely impossible to compile except in the most anecdotal ways, but that does not render the proposition—that a black Romeo or female Prospero(a) does not speak in particular ways to corresponding parts of the audience—false. The nature of such association and its claims to ownership of, or even empowerment through, Shakespeare, must similarly be evaluated on the same case-by-case basis. That said, there must be some value to the idea that segments of the population who have traditionally been excluded from Shakespeare feel able to claim it, not simply as a cultural trophy but as something which they are entitled to own, interrogate and evaluate for themselves, on the strength of seeing roles played by people apparently like them.

One of the dangers of non-traditional casting is that audiences are prone to discount it as a theatrical effect, a mere convention of the show which they attempt to see past, because they assume it a gimmick (aesthetic or political). So while the actuality of the bodies work on the audiences' senses, the audience's conscious minds attempt to overwrite those sensory impressions as irrelevant. In the case of the photonegative *Othello*, the casting became merely a device which foregrounded a star actor in a role he wouldn't otherwise be able to play, while in the Globe's *Shrew*, the casting reinforced the production's comic element which seemed merely to invert a pantomime cross-dressing tradition without acquiring more gravitas along the way. Gravitas was not a problem for Peter Sellars' 1994 *Merchant of Venice*, in which racial crosscasting was used to invoke the tension of the recent L.A. riots (Venice here was a contemporary Venice Beach, not Venice, Italy), and the play's ethnic preoccupation with Jewishness was significantly expanded. The play's Jews were played by African Americans, the Venetians were Hispanic, Portia and her retinue were Asian, and only Launcelot and his father (who doubled as the duke) were Caucasian. The production, which opened at the Goodman theatre in Chicago before travelling to New York and London, used multimedia projection, pre-recorded video clips, and simultaneously fed live capture, and aspects of the show met with critical approval. James Loehlin, writing for *Theatre Journal*, said that Sellars's "reading of the play 'as what happens when mercantile attitudes are applied to personal relationships' was dead on target, and the contemporary L.A. setting thoroughly appropriate" (94) but had grave concerns about the show's actual execution. The production was "heavy with ideas and inventiveness, but painfully slow, badly acted, and dependent on a large-scale interpretive conceit that was only intermittently revealing" (94). While Loehlin commends the constant presence of the three caskets (here literally coffins) and the trial scene's use of footage of the Rodney King beating—"a devastating moment, true to the play, true to Sellars's vision of contemporary America, and to the actual situation of an upper-class white audience confronted by black anger"—he felt the production finally failed as theatre. The show, "in spite of its powerful conception, was profoundly unengaging and excruciatingly slow." The "television-trained" actors were dwarfed by and uncomfortable on the set, and their microphones further separated them from the audience and made it difficult to tell who was speaking. The actress playing Portia gave what Loehlin calls a "cripplingly bad performance," emotionally overwrought and "devoid of the wit that makes the least attractive of Shakespeare's heroines bearable." Even interesting ideas can be subverted by shoddy execution.

For all its concerns with race and ethnicity, one of the oddities of the production was its treatment of the Jewish issue as something from the past, an ancient image of racial hatred which could be applied elsewhere to other groups, an idea some would find problematic or offensive. It might be argued that Sellars's agenda was finally less about race and more about what Chris Salter calls "the fracturing and reduction of human experience through the media," (135) so the resultant audience estrangement or alienation from all those video screens and glimpses of news footage was perhaps his point, though whether the idea *qua* idea was enough to counter the dissatisfaction felt by an audience who came to see a production of the *Merchant of Venice* is another matter entirely. It should be pointed out that Sellars's adaptive strategies did not operate at the level of text since barely a line was cut, though this paradoxically "pure" approach to the script was one of the contributing factors in the show's four-hour running time and came in for serious criticism, most devastatingly through audiences voting with their feet: David Richards, writing for the *New York Times*, claimed that on the night he saw the show two-thirds of the house left at intermission, a phenomenon observed by other reviewers during the show's Chicago run. The *Times* reviewer complained of missing the play's humour, its sense of complex psychology and emotional weight, but recognized a political thrust which stood in some sense outside the play:

> I can't entirely dismiss the production's unconventional fascinations. This cool, splintered view of "The Merchant of Venice" may have no more to do with traditional Shakespeare than a hand-lettered scroll has to do with E-mail, but it does say something disturbing about American malaise in the 1990s... What Mr. Sellars sees happening to society at large—a pulling apart of the races and a general breakdown of humanity—happens to his performers as well, who become less than the sum of their parts. Frequently, a conscious effort is required to match voice and body, face and feeling. You get the impression, after a while—as actors hunch over microphones and their profiles are splashed across the monitors—that you're watching a Congressional investigation into "The Merchant of Venice."
>
> (Richards)

This idea of the production as an investigation into the play rather than a staging of it perhaps suggests a false binary in which there are true productions and there are adaptations, but it does indicate a familiar concern with politically aggressive cross-casting, in which whatever comes across as potentially interesting or provocative does so in spite of the play itself.

At one point in his review, Richards targets Elaine Tse in ways similar to Loehlin, though in terms betraying different assumptions. While Loehlin called Portia "the least attractive of Shakespeare's heroines" Richards calls her "arguably one of Shakespeare's smartest and liveliest heroines." There is, I suppose, much virtue in "arguably." The contrasting assumptions might be polarized on political lines since Portia is central to the trial scene and, in some critical readings, complicit not just in Venice's anti-Semitism but also in a more general racism as her remarks about the Prince of Morroco's "complexion" can be seen to indicate (2.7.79). To persist in seeing her simply as smart and lively willfully sidesteps a political reading, but Richards's complaint that she "has become in Mr. Sellars's interpretation of things a perpetually distraught woman of abiding neuroses" is remarkably similar to Loehlin's who targets the performance as overplayed and psychologically baffling. In each case, the idea of the character and its attendant political implications is subverted by the execution of that character played as a person on stage.

Depending on one's position, of course, this might not matter, and plenty of directors and critics would applaud the elevation of political thrust and contemporary resonance over being perceived as being "true" to the Bard, but there remains the difficulty of navigating audiences whose interest—even if it isn't in Shakespeare per se—still tends to be in story and character as defined broadly by realist drama. Richards' final complaint that Sellars would be more appreciated if he felt more and thought less is surely illustrative of what Brecht would call a bourgeois sensibility, but it also indicates that political effect might be better achieved through other means. Productions which force audiences to rethink what theatre is put a tremendous strain on the content of their productions, a strain which will lead some audiences to discount the production as failed theatre rather than theatre of a different kind. This seems doubly true of Shakespeare where assumptions about what the plays are and what is the source of their abiding worth seem to run contrary to conceptual approaches which are perceived to use the play in pursuit of an idea or aesthetic which comes from elsewhere. Again, the binary is simplistic, but political effect must be measured in its impact on audiences, not on academics who may read the show for political nuance others do not see.

There are, of course, other ways of wrestling with politically difficult Shakespeare. Reviewing a National Theatre production directed by Trevor Nunn five years later, Michael Billington opens his *Guardian* review with a key question and a surprisingly simple answer: "How does one solve the problems inherent in the *Merchant of Venice*? By giving the action a specific emotional and social context" (Billington). Surprisingly, Billington lists Sellars's production as one which did precisely this, though the production he goes on to discuss takes an entirely different approach to such "specific emotional and social context." Nunn's production was crucially realist, a 1930s Venetian café society of suave Christians and a Hebraic subculture in which Shylock is a religiously observant Jew who speaks Yiddish to Jessica. Traditional casting—by which I mean casting actors who seem to be of the ethnicity of the characters they play—reinforces the simpler, more literal approach to the text, but doing so does not strip the production of its political dimension. Robert Smallwood's review of the production includes these telling details:

> Shylock's return home through the revellers to his unanswered front door, his fumbling with his keys, his discovery of Jessica's departure (she had kissed her mother's photograph goodbye, after his earlier exit), were the inevitable prelude to his cracking up at his next appearance. It was the urbane indifference to his grief of Salerio and Solanio that did it. He had greeted them eagerly, as though pleased to have their company. Their mocking callousness produced a version of "Hath not a Jew eyes" that was eager, urgent, intended to be persuasive, and then turned very fierce, though with the tremor of grief beneath, on "shall we not revenge?" his body tense with fury at the years of ill-treatment. It was at this point that Peter de Jersey's Salerio began to part company with Mark Umber's implacably racist Solanio, a move that would show Salerio, by the end of the trial scene, appalled at the behaviour of his fellow Christians and physically restraining the threatened violence of Richard Henders's loathsome Gratiano.
>
> (Smallwood 269)

This sketch of Salerio's psychological journey nicely frames both the socially general and historically conditioned nature of anti-Semitism in the world of the play, but grounds it in the life and attitudes of individuals within the fiction. Such an approach challenges the charge of the play's inevitable and unavoidable anti-Semitism by taking it seriously and grappling with it through the opposite of estranging or alienating the audience, rather inviting them inside the world of the story so that they may understand its characters. Nor does it fall back on generalized humanism in which things like race are incidentals, finally unimportant to the core of the play. Nunn's production may generate more of an emotional response than an intellectual one but that does not necessarily dull its political edge, and it accords more happily (as Richards' review of the Goodman production suggests) with audience expectations about how theatre should affect them. This may produce a less urgent political idea or—and I don't think the loaded and slightly pejorative tone inappropriate—*message*, but if the alternative leaves the theatre two-thirds empty by the end, that is perhaps not a bad thing. Billington's review of the National production concludes thus:

> Nunn presents us with a genuine clash of wills, value-systems and revenge-motifs. You are not asked to sympathise with Henry Goodman's excellent Shylock: you are simply asked to understand him. Goodman also brings to the role a genuine moral gravity masked by ironic humour. Sometimes the director's love of novelistic detail seems a bit excessive... but by giving the play a specific context, Nunn rescues it from fairy tale whimsy or visible anti-Semitism.
>
> Instead what we get is a play about the ubiquity of money, about a world where secular Christian lightness comes up against a fierce Hebraic severity and where the one quality that both sides recognise in each other is the unquenchable thirst for revenge. In short, a challenging and disturbing production.

That "challenging and disturbing" is surely telling, particularly in the context of *rescuing* the show from *visible* anti-Semitism. Context, here, is all. The production's focus, at least from Billington's perspective, is in exploring the play and explaining its various and troubling energies as rooted in a specific social environment, without advocating for a particular take on those energies. I don't think that there is any question that such a production is still political, even if it is not offering an explicit political conclusion.

The three productions utilizing non-traditional casting which I have discussed here all finally struggle to get their political ideas across in ways the audience was prepared to countenance. The last production, Nunn's *Merchant*, might be seen as a stand in for all the other productions of *Merchant*, of *Shrew*, of *Othello* (and, indeed, of *Titus Andronicus*, *Two Gentlemen of Verona*, *Antony and Cleopatra* or any of the other Shakespeare plays which hinge on potentially problematic issues of identity politics) which attempt to navigate the plays' difficult or potentially incendiary politics from the inside and in broadly realist ways. Those which use non-traditional casting were, I think, less successful, though that does not invalidate the strategy for all plays or all audiences, and it is easy to imagine productions where the same devices would have worked better (a photonegative *Othello* with a different lead and a more diverse audience, for instance). What does seem evident, however, is the way that the theatrical dynamic and the audiences in particular—especially their make-up and their expectations—inflected the meaning of these productions in ways which subverted their political agency. Nunn's *Merchant*, and other similarly realist, specific productions, produced a political effect which was less Brechtian, less agitprop, less statement, manifesto or rallying cry, and it worked upon the audience by moving them, perhaps into places they would have refused to go if led by a strictly intellectually or schematic approach. This does not make realist, psychologized Shakespeare more politically effective than more radical approaches to casting, but it is perhaps a useful corrective to the assumption that the opposite is true.

4
"Who talks of my nation?" Challenging the Establishment

If some Shakespeare plays are particularly good grist for the mill of identity politics, others—notably the histories and tragedies—naturally invite association with the politics of statecraft, nationhood, and the power to rule. Few combine these concerns better than the second tetralogy (*Richard II*, *Henry IV part 1*, *Henry IV part 2*, and *Henry V*) with its preoccupation with the getting and maintaining of power in the face of enemies foreign and domestic, and the last play in the sequence is a particular flashpoint for competing ideological views focused through the lens of kingship. As elsewhere, the importance of this play as a consideration of power and an especially British nationalism has been shaped as much by the cultural legacy surrounding the play as by the lines within it, and any consideration of recent productions in political terms must be placed in a larger context, notably the long and potent shadow cast by the film version of *Henry V* made in 1944 by Laurence Olivier.

Olivier won a special Academy Award for serving as the film's producer, director, and actor, and some critics thought it the most successful film version of Shakespeare ever made, particularly in its embrace of cinema's visual elements.[1] There is no question, though, that the positive reception came also in part from the film's apparently heroic celebration of Englishness and martial courage, made doubly potent by the fact that the movie was dedicated to the troops who participated in the D-Day landings the year the film was released. Though the film is not without subtlety, even complexity, Henry is the distillation of an eighteenth- and nineteenth-century tradition of the king as virtuous and chivalric folk hero, his conquest of France (as per the Normandy battles of the same year) more a liberation from dissolute rule than an invasion proper. The movie as a movie also enacted its subject matter, being a triumph of the British film industry in a medium generally dominated by Hollywood.

Whatever the subtleties of the film, the scale of its success and its perceived univocal pro-Henry, pro-British heroic agenda, became—for the latter part of the century—a model of conservatism in opposition to which more radical productions sought to define themselves. As Olivier's film had built on contemporary military events in mainland Europe, British productions of the 1980s grew out of the very different cultural associations with the Falklands War of 1982. The then deeply unpopular Prime Minister, Margaret Thatcher, overcame widespread dissatisfaction with her economic policies by sending a naval task force to expel the Argentinean troops who had occupied a group of sparsely populated islands which, since 1833, have been under British rule. The success of the two-month military campaign fed a nationalist fervour which, coupled with disastrous Labour Party leadership and the all too recent memories of battles with trade unions, led to Thatcher's convincing re-election. Soon after, however, the left's perception of the war as cynical and grubby politicking became ubiquitous in British intellectual and artistic life, shaping a context for *Henry V* as a play about war mongering abroad to distract the populace from problems and ideological division at home.

The play offers multiple reasons for Henry's French campaign, some of them official (the tortuous legal claim that it is the French who are the usurpers and Henry the rightful king), to the secret (the church's decision to promote the cause in order to secure royal support of their position against a massive tax on church property), to the personal (the affront of the Dauphin's tennis balls insult). But well into the campaign the play is careful to show that the national unity Henry is so keen to demonstrate is a fabrication, an official proclamation about the absence of dissent, which attempts to paper over serious internal dispute. There is the murderous squabbling of the Scots, Irish, and Welsh factions for whom the question of nationhood burns particularly hot. There is also the conspiracy of nobles who are prepared to sell their king to the French for money in pursuit of their own factional intrigues which go back to the days of Richard II and his removal from the throne by Henry's father. And there is the deep ambivalence of the actual soldiers about the morality of what they are doing which Henry glimpses in disguise on the eve of Agincourt.

Two British productions from the mid-eighties engaged these elements directly, one directed by Adrian Noble in 1984 and starring a young Kenneth Branagh (who went on to make his own film version of the play five years later), and the other, more aggressively radical, directed by Michael Bogdanov in 1986. Noble's production was roughly medieval in setting but possessed enough anachronistic details (flashlights, for instance) and a set which reinforced a sense of the presentational that some critics perceived a Brechtian element which was both contemporary and somehow outside the fiction of the story. This was emphasized by the chorus figure, played by a caustically sardonic Ian McDiarmid, who was always on stage but was never acknowledged by the other actors. The result was a kind of frame, ever present, distancing, and sceptical, which qualified Branagh's earnest, likeable king (Loehlin 89).[2] Noble's churchmen were consummate politicians, and some of the royal court were thuggish, while the low characters (Pistol, Bardolph, and Nym) suggested a sense of both pettiness and personal tragedy. The oft cut execution of Bardolph was brought on stage and performed brutally in front of the resolute but devastated king: a powerful indictment of the hard realities of war, but one which attested to their personal costs for Henry himself. As James Loehlin shrewdly observes, such moments allowed Noble "to have his cake and eat it too," in that the production showed the horrors of war while making the king as much its victim as its instigator (94). Henry's order to kill the French prisoners (a moment cut from Branagh's subsequent film) produced a scene of horrific carnage, but the overall effect was ambiguous. The production confronted the horrors of war, without denouncing their necessity, and through the grit and blood it showed a species of heroism, quite different from Olivier's, more humanized and mentally scarred, but not without value. For some, the production was finally politically noncommittal, and newspaper reviews which applauded it often professed radically different senses of its political meaning. The overall staging and the ironic chorus suggested the cynical machinery of power, but Branagh's heartfelt and charismatic king—especially likeable in the wooing scene at the end—still permitted a heroic, even nationalist reading.

Not so with Bogdanov's production two years later for his and Michael Pennington's fledgling English Shakespeare Company performed as the climax of a sequence beginning with both parts of *Henry IV*. Where Noble had presented an essentially sympathetic Henry doing difficult things in the interests of his country, Bogdanov gave us a king in Michael Pennington who was a self-serving and vicious imperialist, his sole goal being to maintain and expand his power base. He did so by exploiting the worst, most jingoistic aspects of a debased nationalism, his army a blood-thirsty rabble of cutthroats who bore "Fuck the Frogs" banners and sang "'ere we go, 'ere we go, 'ere we go" with the voices of soccer hooligans. That last was as timely a piece of business as any reference to the Falklands war. In 1985, the Popplewell Committee's report on the death of a 14-year-old boy at a soccer match in May said the match had been more like the battle of Agincourt, while later that same month 39 Juventus fans died at Heysel stadium trying to escape Liverpool supporters, an event which led to the ban of English clubs from European competition for five years, by which time the Heysel disaster had been dwarfed by the 96 killed during a game at Hillsborough. As was observed by sociologists of the day, the sudden increase in soccer-related violence grew out of the very nationalism which had been stoked by the Falklands, fuelled by poverty, joblessness, and a resultant gang identity. Some went so far as to say that the aggressive disregard for others grew directly out of Mrs. Thatcher's brand of free-market competition and rapacious self-interest.[3] Hooligans, for Bogdanov, represented the clumsy and obvious culture of brutality, bigotry, greed, and xenophobia whose more polished surfaces were called capitalism and patriotism.

In this and other details of set and costume, the production was aggressively contemporary, the battles fought with tanks and Sterling submachine guns, the court assembled like a board meeting, the soldiers looting the corpses and tossing their belongings into shopping carts. When the soldiers wrapped themselves in Union Jacks for another chorus of " 'ere we go, 'ere we go, 'ere we go" during the naming of the dead, the crass and thoughtless instincts of the hooligan rendered all talk of God fighting "for us" absurd, even blasphemous. Here and elsewhere, the hooligan army evoked the skinheads of the far right National Front.

The French were effete, trapped in a perpetual thirties garden party, anachronisms to be swept away by a new and ruthless pragmatism. Pennington's king, by contrast, was a savvy and cynical politician throughout, smug, wilfully unlikeable, barking orders at his underlings, sometimes even threatening them with a weapon. This was bare-faced power, unapologetic and unredeemable, and critics—at least those who saw the production when it first opened—were quick to recognize it as such, whether or not they found such a reading sympathetic. Bogdanov and Pennington, as is not uncommon, claimed that what they were doing was drawing Shakespeare's message to the fore, not rewriting it, and the resultant production was a necessary corrective to the (to their mind) simple-minded heroic readings of the past, a reading perhaps evoked by the plaintive strains of Blake's Jerusalem which vied with the mindless hooligan chants. It was noted by some that the productions' socialist politics were undermined by an attitude to the lower class characters which was almost comically condescending, reducing them to clowns with regional accents (Pistol was a Geordie), caricatures which called into question Bogdanov's critique of the ruling elite. It might be offered in opposition to such a view that such marginalizing of regional dialect was common in Shakespeare (and in British theatre and television more generally) until well into the nineties, and that a certain contempt for the lower social orders commonly (albeit problematically) coexists within a political philosophy which understands the circumstances which create such cultural and economic demographics.

But the politics of the production began to unravel when it went on tour, a contingency which had always been intended and was built into both its spare set and its funding streams. The English Shakespeare Company had been founded as a way of extending the radical politics of what Bogdanov had done at the Royal Shakespeare Company and the National Theatre, giving him a platform from which he might target the reactionary politics of the day and of Thatcher's government in particular. In this, the Falklands war, monetarist policy, the axing of funding for arts and social programmes, and the resultant ravaging of regional economies and communities, all stood as shaping targets for what the new company would attack. Some of these concerns were clearly visible in the production's run at the Old Vic, but the show was contractually obligated to play at the Royal Alex in Toronto as well, and this—as Ric Knowles points out—is where fissures appear in the company's political logic.[4]

No allowances were made for the difference between the English and Canadian audiences, the production reproducing at the Royal Alex what it had done at the Old Vic. The Toronto audiences, according to reviews, didn't understand the British regional accents. They didn't get the joke on Pistol's shirt: "Never Mind the Bollocks, Here comes Pistol," seeing instead of a reference to an iconically subversive punk band only the vaguely amusing Britishism "bollocks" (the meaning of which is often mistaken in North America to mean "bullshit" a la *bullocks*). Representations of the police which Bogdanov intended to resemble Thatcherite thugs of the type who had lined the front lines of the miners' strike rallies, were read as "bobbies on bicycles," and other elements of the production which had evoked subversion and danger back at the Old Vic were here transformed into the quaint echoes of Merry England. Gadshill (in the *Henry IV* plays) sported an oversized Mohawk which might have simply been another punk fashion statement in London, but in Canada seemed to arbitrarily and purposelessly evoke indigenous people. The soccer hooligan associations were largely meaningless for this audience, and anyone who might have been stirred to see something of their own underclass status in the show wouldn't have been able to afford the tickets anyway.⁵ Most troublingly of all, perhaps, it was money from the owners of the Toronto theatre which financed not only the production but also the purchase and refurbishment of the Old Vic, a fact which gives real weight to Knowles' charge that the production was finally perpetrating the kind of colonialist capitalism which the show was ostensibly targeting. The Toronto audiences left (often at intermission) bored and confused, something that—in a final act of colonial condescension—the director dismissed as indicating their lack of cultural sophistication. What French Canadians made of the "Fuck the Frogs" banner, one can only speculate...

Political theatre, as we have observed, is not simply about what happens on stage. Meaning is made by the audience, and audiences are constructed geographically, culturally, and economically. Failure to take that into account destabilizes a production's political agenda, perhaps even—as Knowles would argue—exposing it as, if not actually fraudulent, then inadequately thought through.

The early years of the twenty-first century changed Western ideas of war, particularly in the United States which grappled with the implications of the September 11th attacks of 2001, and the various forms of military action in Iraq and Afghanistan which followed them. In the latter years of that first decade those military concerns, coupled with political sea changes and a lengthy recession, brought forth several productions with topical roots. *Henry V* continued to be a lightning rod for politically topical production, as was evidenced by the 2003 Royal National Theatre staging starring Adrian Lester as Henry and directed by Nicholas Hytner. This was a modern dress show which made direct allusion to the then concurrent war in Iraq, the clergy brandishing what—to English audiences—resembled the "dodgy dossiers" supposedly proving Saddam Hussein's possession of weapons of mass destruction which the Blair government used to build popular support for British involvement in the campaign. This was an expressly anti-war production, its common soldiers weary and dispirited, its generals—particularly the king himself—slick and pragmatic, their exploits broadcast on television screens by embedded reporters, except when those exploits (such as the massacre of the French prisoners) needed to be kept conveniently off camera. It was a grubby, alienating production largely praised for its cleverness and effectiveness, though critics like Michael Billington missed the play's more nuanced approach, even as he applauded the political sentiment (*The Guardian*). Yet Charles Spencer, reviewing for the more conservative *Daily Telegraph*, had nothing but praise for the production, in spite of its lack of patriotism, and commended the casting of Lester, who is black, as a further—positive—echo of Britain's multicultural present. It might be argued, of course, that the deeply unpopular Iraq war was a comparatively easy target in England, as is perhaps evidenced by the way that both political spectrums embraced the production's core message, but the show succeeded in making the play feel imminent and fresh. Many critics applauded its obvious relevance to the time and admired the way a largely realist production could assert its political point through direct contemporary analogy.

Henry V was not the only play which proved politically usable in the early years of the new millennium. *Macbeth* also enjoyed a topical resurgence in a flurry of new productions and adaptations. Among the most interesting were a cluster of overtly satirical and subversive pieces titled *Macbush* (2003/4), a grotesquely violent RSC production directed by Conall Morrison (2007), a pair of high-profile international touring shows—one faintly Stalinist from Britain, one high-tech and anti-American from Poland (2008), and one staged by the African American Shakespeare Project which rethought the contemporary refashioning of the play in terms of contemporary black culture (2009). All were overtly, even aggressively political in ways which emerged from and responded to the current zeitgeist, though their success as political theatre varied tremendously.

To begin with the earliest, the *Macbush* "stagings" (and I use that cautiously ambiguous term advisably) varied tremendously in form and genre since they were not coordinated by any single entity but self-generated all over the world in response to what was seen by many as the violent pursuit of its interests at home and abroad by the second Bush administration. Some of these, such as Michael Hettinger's *Tragedy of Macbush* in Oakland, California (2003), were rescripted tellings of Shakespeare's tragedy, reshaped to suit the company's political critique, while others—such as the demonstrations which took place close to Dromoland Castle, Ireland, while Bush was there for the US/EU summit, were political pageantry and street theatre. In that latter instance, elements of the play like the walking forest, the witches, and quoted lines from the text were invoked iconographically to critique US military policy in a form of outdoor demonstration.

Todd Landon Barnes has shown the way such performances enact a political reclaiming of Shakespeare from an administration which—paradoxically—had invested considerable resources into Shakespeare-supportive arts grants: the National Endowment for the Arts's Shakespeare in American Communities project which toured productions all over the country to venues which, thanks to a fiscal partnership with the Department of Defence, included military bases.[6] It was *Macbeth* which was performed for the military. The project was clearly premised on an assumption of Shakespeare's politically conservative and authoritative cultural position, even, ironically, as Shakespeare was being used to subvert the political status quo by other organizations. Barnes points out that the superficial binary which seems to emerge from these two conflicting attitudes to the play in performance are not, in fact, sustainable, the most radically subversive and marginalized approaches of the various *Macbush* productions potentially engendering reactionary audience responses, while the conservatism at the heart of the National Endowment for the Arts (NEA)'s agenda could also be derailed or inverted in the actuality of production. In the Alabama Shakespeare Festival's NEA funded tours of military bases, for instance, the inherent improvization necessary for adjusting to new audiences and performance spaces created an essentially unscripted quality that separated the actual performances from the official mandate which authorized them in the first place. More to the point, perhaps, what active military personnel made of scenes of combat violence and corrupt, ambitious leadership is impossible to say with certainty. As Barnes points out, the Washington officials who dreamed up the project in the first place and championed it as a model of conservative cultural authority never saw a single production.

In the United Kingdom, the Royal Shakespeare Company mounted a vaguely Balkans-inspired contemporary *Macbeth*, directed by Conall Morrison, which was widely condemned for the production's casual and graphic savagery. What was supposed to throw light on a military culture of violence (the production opened with an extra textual scene in which Macbeth slaughtered a group of women and children who had barricaded themselves into a room) was attacked as subordinating any psychological or political subtlety to a single, reductive concept. Moreover, this Macbeth began so steeped in blood that he had no moral journey, a fact which rendered lines about his being too full of the milk of human kindness simply absurd. He was a puppet of the omnipresent witches (resurrected victims of that first massacre), thereby stripping him of both agency and responsibility, all in service of the large and general point that military violence and the horrors of war beget more of the same. The world of the production lacked specific associations, so the overall effect was of a generalized moral, offered up in ways designed to shock, titillate or offend. Any specific political point was, to my mind, lost in the resulting crass and noisy shuffle.

Two touring productions reached New York in 2008, one from the Chichester Festival (directed by Rupert Goold and starring Patrick Stewart and Kate Fleetwood), the other a massive cinematic extravaganza from Poland. The Chichester production (which gave rise to a well-received 2010 film) anchored its study of totalitarian evil in what was generally considered a late forties or early fifties Soviet context but was hailed less for its political angle and more for the psychological studies which developed within it. This was where the specificity of the production lay, and though the show was marked with newsreel footage of military parades evoking the scale of the power the Macbeths commanded, the result was read in terms of an existential study of people facing up to the horror of their own choices.[7] Stewart's Macbeth was almost Hamletic in its mental richness and its hallmark was a kind of ordinariness that transcended the large-scale politics of the setting so that the scene most commented on was probably that in which he ordered the death of Banquo while making himself a sandwich in the kitchen.

Such a production emphasized the banality of political evil rather than seeking contemporary analogues to make a more specific point, while TR Warszawa's production, directed by Grzegorz Jarzyna did the opposite. This show used the full range of large-scale multimedia effects to create a version of the play (in Polish with projected English subtitles) in which an expressly American war machine murdered its way through the middle east. Iraq dominated the production, though there were glimpses of Chechnya and the Balkans as well, but the most insistent associations seemed to be less political than they were cinematic, with critics seeing echoes of *Black Hawk Down* and even *Blade Runner* (Ryzik). The production was massive and expensive, a purpose-built amphitheatre involving various huge projection surfaces constructed in a roofless nineteenth-century tobacco warehouse so that the Manhattan landscape provided a pointed backdrop to the action, the final effect being—as one critic observed—that the show's message was being delivered "from the belly of the beast" (Stasio). That message concerned a robotic Macbeth's pursuit of power and a military campaign in which praying Moslem insurgents were assaulted by rappelling marines from helicopters, the terrorist leader gleefully beheaded on stage, and prisoners in Arab garb were tortured in dungeons by Coke swilling Americans. The production was a commercial success, but the abiding critical response was to the visual scale of the spectacle and its extremely broad brush political approach. No one saw much in the way of nuance or subtlety (and in this comparisons were often made to the Goold/Stewart production, always to TR Warszawa's detriment), and the vaguely complimentary adjective "cinematic" often turned into the less positive "comic book."[8] *The New York Times* review sums up the problem nicely:

> The blood-soaked circus is intermittently fun to watch—the "what next?" factor has its value as a suspense generator—but for all the lurid sex, gunfire and madcappery this Polish production, directed by Grzegorz Jarzyna, is ultimately tedious and uninvolving. It's "Macbeth" made over as a contemporary action movie, a "Macbeth" for those who think Shakespeare gummed up a great yarn with all that poetry when he could have been showing us the tasty murders he stubbornly kept offstage.
>
> (Isherwood)

What is clear here is that the political agenda is seen as in some senses at odds with what Shakespeare's play does well, and not just in terms of the kind of psychological study so applauded in the Goold/Stewart production. Part of the problem is that the content of the play was finally seen as not well suited to the politics of the production and that the two were lashed together without much concern for how they would support each other. The *Times* critic, for instance, observes that *Macbeth* is finally not really a war play—though it does involve war—as say, *Henry V* is, so much of the production's emphasis felt extraneous to the core story, the director's agenda and the play's concerns straining against each other in ways finally serving neither. The splashy visuals became, it seems, ends in themselves, and though some audience members came away impressed by the experience, the production's much-touted political approach went oddly undiscussed by the critics, taken as self-evident but not particularly productive in terms of ideas or expressly political responses of a less conscious kind. Indeed, one might argue that the very awe induced by the cinematic effects mitigated against the political content, producing not outrage—as was intended—but a species of pleasure growing, ironically, out of the theatrical and aesthetic equivalent of the "shock and awe" tactics which characterized Bush's invasion of Iraq.

Familiar concerns thus surface as we consider the political ramifications of these various productions. The ones which were able to convey a clear and effective subversion—notably the *MacBush* activist events, though one might include TR Warszawa as well—did so for sympathetic audiences, but did not so much stage the play as use its cultural valences to make a fairly general statement about political ambition and its cynical use of violence as a tool. The play was not intended as a locus of political discourse so much as it was a flag, albeit one which flew usefully counter to the Bush administration's own assumptions about Shakespeare. The NEA touring shows seem far more ambiguous in their political effects and the show which was generally considered the most successful—the Goold/Stewart—was seen as playing character over politics.

Before we leap to the familiar conclusion that Shakespeare will always seem to be more about individual psyches than large-scale political forces—either because that's just how the plays are written or because audiences expect no less from the Bard and the grand humanist tradition he stands for—we should probably stop to scrutinize that character/politics binary. The problem with both the TR Warszawa and the *MacBush* approach is that it suggests that if we aren't thinking in terms of banner moments of the punchiest and most unequivocal statements, then we aren't doing politics. *Macbeth* the play, however, is rooted in the opposite, in moral and political ambiguity, in nuance, in private horror, and in equivocation—one of the driving concerns of the play—in which truth and utterance enjoy a shifting and unstable relationship. As some critics of the TR Warszawa production suggested, the core concerns of the play don't easily mesh with the company's bullhorn approach and the play had to be reduced, flattened out to get them even on the same page. By contrast the Goold/Stewart production in wrestling with the play's essentially domestic brand of politics (and by that I mean both national rather than international and located in a private household) foregrounded not the machinery of power so much as the people who run it. Such a show does not—contrary to the Brechtian tradition—have much to say about the larger social forces which shape such people, but it does offer a critique of the cruel and petty power-broking which culture veils with majesty. It does not offer contemporary analogues as TR Warszawa or the English Shakespeare Company did, but that does not reduce the production to a supposedly "timeless" character-driven study on the nature of evil. As with the NEA's travelling *Macbeth* and its inherent improvizational quality, it is impossible to generalize about what connections audiences made (however subconsciously) to contemporary events, and it could well be that the vaguely Soviet setting functioned—as such historical gestures often do—to facilitate contemporary echoes in ways more productive than the heavier handed schematics of TR Warszawa. The United States was, perhaps, as polarized by Bush's foreign policies as it has been since the Civil War, and the left and right had precious little common ground. TR Warszawa spoke to one wing only (or tried to), while the Chichester production seemed to inhabit a middle ground by virtue of its non-confrontational political frame, but who knows what political effects were facilitated by being in a position where audiences actually watched and listened rather than simply cheering or jeering according to the extent to which they agreed with the production's insistent manifesto. I am not trying to assert that all productions of Shakespeare are necessarily political (though in a limited and not terribly helpful sense, of course, they are), but I do want to extend Barnes' assertion that political effect is created in the minds of the audience and is therefore plural, contradictory, and irreducible to what the company say—or think—they are doing. I also think that while such conventional shows like that from the Chichester Festival are working according to a very different theatrical model than Boal's Brazilian street theatre, such a show may be closer to the spirit of collective inquiry and audience involvement in the making of meaning which Boal favoured than more aggressively political productions which set out to lecture their audience. These productions are also a study in how the full materiality of theatre informs its political meanings since we can see in each case that the political reading of the play, the ostensible approach utilized by the director or the company, was complicated or undermined by the local specifics of the actual performance conditions in much the way Knowles sees Bogdanov's *Henry V* problematized in its Canadian residency.

All the conventional *Macbeth* productions discussed above (as opposed to the more heavily adaptive *MacBush* agit prop pieces) were touring shows. I'd like to close this chapter by considering one more *Macbeth* production which was deliberately locally rooted in ways which altered its political affect along lines, perhaps, closer to Boal's model. One of the beneficiaries of the aforementioned NEA project, Shakespeare in American Communities, was the San Francisco-based African American Shakespeare Company, whose provocative motto is "envisioning the classics with color." (About Us). That "envisioning" seems to me telling, suggestive as it is of a deliberate reimagining, a choice which seeks to encounter the plays largely as they have been known (rather than in radically transformed adaptations) but rethought and examined through the lenses of race, colour, and ethnicity. In this case, *MacB: The Macbeth Project* (2009) utilized Shakespeare's text with a few minor alterations (mainly proper nouns) but was set in the expressly local world of a black music empire, with all the trappings and logic of "gangsta" culture, hip hop and its particular Bay Area form, "hyphy." Any black *Macbeth* production inevitably evokes Welles' famous 1936 "Voodoo" *Macbeth*, but instead of being a pastiche of white impressions of black culture (though one which could claim a brand of activism in its own day), this one enacted a black community's laying claim to the core of Shakespeare's story on their own terms.[9] References to horses were changed to cars (specifically that so-called urban assault vehicle, the Hummer), Duncan became industry mogul "Top Dog," the witches were a Destiny's Child-style trio, the production was shot through with drug references, and the banquet scene was reimagined as a music video shoot.[10] Costumes seemed to evoke a number of quite specific but eclectic moments in hip hop history, and the show seemed to offer, among other things, a consideration of the uneasy, sometimes violent and finally destructive relationship between the music's historical roots and its corporate manipulation. Significantly, however, though fights were visceral and well staged, the production was (in pointed contrast to the gory savagery of the TR Warszawa production) deliberately bloodless, and anything that might be graphic on stage was kept off. The violence of the world invoked by the production was well known, and the company was careful not to glamorize it or reduce it to horror-film spectacle.

It goes without saying that the power of such a production lies not in its evocation or critique of national and international political issues, but in its enactment of a cultural world which is not just familiar to its audience but which in some ways surrounds it. The play, while retaining its complexity and richness, is made new in the image of its audience, thereby facilitating a different kind of affective association. The politics of such an approach become clearer in the light of the production's subsequent tour, partly because of where it toured and how. Rather than crossing the ocean, the African American Shakespeare Company (AASC)'s tour stayed strictly local, playing at schools, many of them catering specifically to students identified as "at risk" of failing out or worse. Instead of simply remounting the production, the tour played a series of interactive games with the students centred on the play, followed by a version of the production reduced to play in three-quarters of an hour. What happened in the school workshops resembles the work of Augusto Boal more directly than any Shakespeare I have discussed thus far, centring as they did on participatory games which grew out of the students' own culture, particularly out of music and dance. These then primed the way for a production to which the students had been granted a particular and specific brand of ownership. Todd Landon Barnes describes what happened in one such workshop as follows:

> Each time a student participated in any way, either by answering questions or by sharing personal stories of moments when, like Macbeth, they made bad choices, Young [the AASC performer/teacher]

would hand that student a raffle ticket. Students who performed for the class were rewarded with a bag of cookies. Students performed vocabulary words from the *Macbeth* text (of which Willow had a mere five copies), translating the black-and-white text into movement and action. This aspect of the AASC's performance pedagogy opened up the polysemy contained within its stated goal of "envisioning the classics with color." The classics-color binary seemed at once to contain a multicultural imperative alongside a desire to breathe color, life and movement into an inert black-and-white textuality. How do students specializing in the "hip" and the "hop" engage with the radical alterity of a moribund text that seems both uncool and unmoving (both physically and affectively)? Young's solution was to encourage students to make Shakespeare's characters "come alive." In this way, her engagement with at-risk youth looked less like a project of juvenile rehabilitation and more like a project of theatrical reincarnation (466).

When one student had to somehow perform "sovereignty," Barnes goes on to say, he used a monologue from the play but incorporated it into his body in such a way to enact not simply a character but a social system:

> As his curled body cursed his king and glorified his own labor, his performance seemed to express his situation as the central figure in a Russian doll of political and aesthetic projects. Instead of simply enacting sovereignty by playing the king, this student enacted the idea of sovereignty by presenting the *relationships* and *labor* constituting sovereign power. His monologue, which interrogated notions of credit, theft and profit, seemed to mix commentary on the "CEO rights" and royalties of *MacB* with the rights and limits of sovereignty explored in *Macbeth*.

The workshop concluded with the spontaneous group dance-driven hyphy performance in which the students contribute their own mechanized actions which intersect in the creation of a unified, organic machine. This creative, free-form performative play celebrates their individuality even as it affirms and builds a community, tapping into what the students are, what they can do, rather than defining them by their social or educational inadequacies. In this the Shakespeare component looms large, because it could manifest those very failures, one of those unwieldy markers of the dominant culture which serves to keep them out, down or otherwise on the margins. In bringing together the play (recast and imagined to invite direct association) with such opportunities to flex their own idiosyncratic intellectual and creative muscle, the AASC workshop production creates not that familiar chimera relevance, but ownership, a sense that Shakespeare (or anything else with hegemonic associations) might actually be theirs after all and might be made to speak their ideas, their concerns, their values. Subversive political theatre need not be simply ideologically subversive. It might also be constructive at the local level. As such, political theatre cannot be defined solely as offering commentary on or critique of current socio-economic conditions or military actions, and must also be allowed to serve as a form of empowerment in itself.

5
"Let him be Caesar": Representing Politics

While all Shakespeare plays might be considered political or might be made so in performance, others simply are political in the very marrow of their bones. One of these is *Julius Caesar*, a historically rooted play about conspiracy, assassination, the manipulation of popular opinion, and the military outgrowth of political action. This is a play whose very blood—that which gives it life and motion—is politics. Yet the play has a vexed performance history and is widely considered to be flawed as the starting point of a piece of theatre which audiences will flock to: it is almost completely without humour, it has only two small female roles, it is low on visual spectacle and, most damning of all, suffers from the structural problem of the title character dying midway through the play, after which the story seems to lose its drive and dramatic appeal, ending in squabbles and piecemeal combat scenes populated by characters who were not part of the play's first acts. These are valid complaints, and I have no interest in sweeping them under the rug here, looming large as they inevitably do in the mind of any director bold enough to tackle the play on stage. They are complaints, of course, which have not harmed the play's utility in the classroom (where its lack of bawdy humour has actually increased its durability), but its use in schools has only furthered the play's aura of dust and dryness on stage.

It need not be thus, of course, but as I move into a consideration of how this play has been approached on stage politically, it is worth bearing in mind that any production has to balance a sense of what is intellectually interesting or challenging with the emotional or visceral charge of theatre to grab its audience, to pull them in and to—there is no getting around the word—*entertain* them. While some people—especially those who live under oppressive or totalitarian regimes—may go to the theatre for expressly political reasons, most do not, and for them the fear as they step into a production of *Julius Caesar* is not that it will be radically subversive or conservative but that it will be hard to follow or—worse—boring. And in truth, it often is. Partly the problem (other than those already listed) is the play's brand of politics, which is often assumed to be talky and cerebral, archaic not just in setting but in the very manner of its politics which hinge on aristocratic men mulling over issues of honour and nobility, and the very act which should make the play exciting—a murder—is made remote by history and its isolation from the way most of us think of politics today. In order to overcome such prejudices, successful productions have to find ways to make the political world of the play not just plausible or "relevant," but urgent and immediate. Brecht is helpful here because he articulated the false binary at the heart of attacks on epic or dialectical theatre: the assumption that theatre can be either instructive *or* entertaining. Not only did Brecht reject such a notion, he also demonstrated how the attitude belittles both elements of the binary. "Surprising as it may seem," he wrote, "the object is to discredit learning by presenting it as not enjoyable. But in fact of course it is enjoyment that is being discredited by this deliberate suggestion that one learns nothing from it" (Brecht 60).

Politically, *Caesar* is a tricky play, because it does not clearly present a coherent agenda or message. It represents an assassination but shows comparatively little of the kind of autocratic behaviour that would make the killing of the dictator seem genuinely necessary or desirable. The motives of the conspirators are discussed at length, but what we actually see does little to make their actions unequivocally right, and Mark Antony's subsequent victories (first rhetorical, then military) prevent a clear sense of the murder achieving much of anything. Some critics have seen the play as endorsing an Elizabethan world view that finally demonizes the conspirators for attempting to upset a natural order, and though this seems to me reductive as a reading it is undeniable that the play does not clearly champion either side.[1] While this makes for great (and typically Shakespearean) richness of character and complexity of ideas and issues, it doesn't clearly lend itself to the broad brush of agit prop political theatre without significant retooling. Claus Von Stauffenberg, who in 1944 placed a bomb under Hitler's desk, was arrested with a copy of the play on his person, in which Brutus's speeches had been underlined, but Jurgen Fehling had staged the play in Berlin in 1940 to acclaim from prominent Nazis. The play might be read in a dictatorship as dangerously subversive, but it might also be considered the opposite. The play was, for instance, considered a touchstone for Nelson Mandela's African National Congress (ANC) during their fight against South African apartheid, but when Mandela was in prison, the speech he underlined and signed as befitting his situation ("Cowards die many times before their deaths, the valiant never taste of death but once") belonged not to the conspirators but to Caesar himself. In other words, while the play as text provides politically potent moments, *Julius Caesar* in its entirety tends to equivocate, and this makes it far more difficult for theatrical production to take a univocal political stance.

The forum scene of *Julius Caesar*, in which Brutus speaks to the people to justify his hand in the assassination of Caesar and then Mark Antony—in a much longer address—proceeds to turn the crowd against Brutus and the conspirators, is a study in the power of rhetoric and is (usually) the dramatic climax of the play on stage. As with the representation of the masses in Shakespeare's later Roman play, *Coriolanus*, there is much in the forum scene which—depending on one's reading or the approach of the production—might make politically subversive critics uneasy. The crowd, according to conventional wisdom, are naïve, self-interested, and fickle. They fail to see the extent to which they are being manipulated, first by Brutus of whom they are initially sceptical and then by Mark Antony who is able not merely to win them over, but to invert their attitude to the conspirators entirely, whipping them into a furious mutiny which—as the scene in which Cinna the poet is murdered shows—is indiscriminately bloodthirsty. The individual members of the crowd are not what Flavius called them at the beginning of the play, "blocks," "stones," "worse than senseless things." They actually feel too much, are too easily stoked with anger in ways that change them from an audience of individuals to a murderous mob. It is a disconcerting representation of the general public, and in the course of the play's stage history, it has been navigated in various ways. I would like to look at some of these approaches to see how their differing methodologies create different political effects from the same textual material.

There is an aesthetic and logistical problem with staging crowd scenes. Where do you put the people if they are to be addressed at length by characters on stage? What do the crowds look like and how do they behave, particularly when the production needs to ensure that Brutus or Antony can be seen and heard?[2] Are they professional actors (which is expensive) or extras (which runs the risk of amateurism)? Are they the theatre audience itself, and if so how does a director avoid the feel of fakery when that audience is supposed to shout in response to what the actors on stage say?

The early modern playhouse was, of course, a very different kind of place than most theatres today, and it is easy to imagine two differing approaches to the forum scene which might have been staged at the Globe. One involves the use of the stage's upper level or balcony by the principal speaker, while the lower stage area was filled with those playing the crowd. This method would make sense out of the text's implication that Brutus speaks from a pulpit or that Antony must "come down" to interact with the crowd. An alternate possibility is that the actors who played the speaking members of the crowd were dotted around the house itself, mingling with the actual theatre audience so that their shouts seemed to come from a much larger group of which each spectator was a member. Given the famously unruly attitude of that day-lit audience, it is not inconceivable that such a crowd would indeed respond vocally to what they heard, led perhaps by the actors assigned to be their mouthpieces.[3]

But after the restoration, English theatre gradually became a more sedate place and the days of actor/audience interaction steadily diminished. As a result, the next phase of the play's production history tended to see the Roman populace as curiously irrelevant, the play being conceived as a study in Roman nobility (in both senses of that word). In the eighteenth and nineteenth century, for instance, the key speeches by Brutus and Mark Antony were generally delivered as rhetorical set pieces presented directly to the house, often concluding with a curtain call to celebrate the actor's delivery. Such productions foregrounded the monologues as oratorical exercises, and they were delivered in silence because they had had no audience but those sitting respectfully still off-stage in the theatre itself. As a solution to the problem of representing the people of Rome on stage, this was at best a partial solution, one which eliminated the actual bodies of the crowds and turned the dramatic moment into a kind of school room exercise. It is, perhaps, not surprising that the forum scenes were not then considered the thrilling apotheosis of the play, the most theatrically popular scene being the later "tent scene" (4.3), in which Brutus and Cassius argued over their conduct of the war. Clearly this is another instance in which aesthetic sensibilities, modes of performance, even theatre architecture itself had direct consequences for the political ramifications of a dramatic moment. In political terms, however, the eighteenth-century approach to the play as a series of rhetorical set pieces did not simply reduce the dramatic aspect of the play and turn it into a kind of auditory spectacle; it also reinforced an essentially conservative notion of the political world in which the only people of consequence were the aristocrats who existed in a kind of social vacuum as they dictated the rise and fall of their nation state. Removing the civilian population from the play doesn't just silence them; it makes them irrelevant, ciphers with no political significance or power.

By the end of the nineteenth century, Victorian theatre had fallen in love with a pictorial realism leading to massive casts which peopled the plays. In the case of *Julius Caesar*, this meant large numbers of Roman extras costumed according to the latest archaeological evidence, going about their daily lives on stage as the play opened. What might have been simply romantically pseudo historicist tableau was given an edge by the German Meiningen company which toured Europe and the United States in the 1880s, whose extras were real actors trained to think of themselves as individuals with thoughts and feelings of their own. These crowds were more volatile than the token presences common in *Caesar* productions before, and the key orators had to work hard to win them over, often taking a long time before they could even be heard. The result was not simply an escalation of the plausibility of the dramatic action. It created a sense of crisis, that electrifying theatrical effect where audiences are momentarily unsure what is going to happen next, however well they know the play. It also, of course, gives real authority to the nameless crowd, reinforcing the notion that for all their skill, Brutus and Antony finally *need* the people, because that is where the real power to run the Empire lies.

The unsettling nature of this power was presented for the first time on the modern stage in Orson Welles's 1937 Mercury Theatre production in New York, a modern dress staging which made overt connection to the then contemporary threat of European Fascism through its costumes, set and lighting effects (modelled on the Nuremberg rallies). This production made the crowds ordinary, modern Americans whose basest impulses were fired by Nazi theatricality, and was the first on record to include the scene which follows the forum oratory, in which we witness the cynically casual murder of Cinna the Poet simply because his name is the same as one of the conspirators. The production saw Brutus as a principled and intellectual liberal who was finally out of his depth in the face of such studied audience manipulation as was being seen on newsreel footage from Germany and Italy, and the crowd scenes were a warning of what might happen elsewhere if the Fascist threat was not met head on.

For much of the twentieth century, this reading of the play as a study in demagoguery and the dangerous manipulation of the populace persisted, often in similarly Fascistic trappings, though the political edge dulled significantly after the Second World War. The play seemed to become, once again, curiously apolitical, safe, a school room exercise in rhetoric, rather than the urgent and anxiously political call to arms it had been for Welles. Ironically, the more productions made direct reference to the then vanquished Nazis, the less insistent the production's political message seemed to be. It took more contemporary analogies and new approaches to staging to rediscover *Caesar*'s political potential. In England in the 1980s, for instance, there were several productions by the Royal Shakespeare Company which clearly saw something of then Prime Minister Margaret Thatcher in Caesar's autocratic dictatorship. These productions, however—and I am thinking particularly of Ron Daniels's 1983 production, Terry Hands's in 1987, and Steven Pimlott's in 1991—struggled to make direct political association, in spite of their programme notes, partly because the settings were historically vague and partly because their Caesars were all pointedly male. This is understandable, of course. Recasting Caesar as a woman would have made the link to the prime minister uncomfortably clear in ways which might have been considered artistically clumsy, reductive, or simply tasteless, particularly after the Brighton bombing of 1984 which targeted her. Direct association with the prime minister might also have endangered state funding of the company which was, at the time, particularly precarious for theatres doing leftist work. Whatever the reason, however, audiences clearly did not see Thatcher herself in these productions, however much the company seemed to find obvious points of contact, and political immediacy had to be evoked in other ways.

Ron Daniels turned to the crowd scenes to find that immediacy, incorporating a projection system so that the funeral orations were magnified through live video capture and splashed onto the upstage wall. This effect created the illusion of simultaneous television broadcast, the funeral orations becoming more obviously a study in political manipulation in its contemporary medium. It was in the early eighties that British politicians—including famously or, in the minds of the old school Labour pundits of the day, infamously—Thatcher herself had begun to utilize image consultants, vocal coaches, and other media-savvy specialists to better craft the impression they made on the television audience. Seeing Mark Antony up there on the screen as he emoted his way through the speech which would turn the crowds into vengeful killers was a neat way of foregrounding the nature of the manipulation and anchoring the Roman past in the British present.

The idea seemed good on paper, but some critics found it alienating, and there were technical problems with the video system so that it was eventually dropped from the production. Other shows from the period fell back on the usual devices: piped crowd noise, operatic choruses speaking in unison like the *Children of the Corn*, isolated handfuls of people trying to look like hundreds. None worked terribly well. The most successful production was probably David Thacker's from 1993, and again theatre architecture was crucial to the logic and political effect of the crowd scenes. Thacker's production was staged at Stratford's The Other Place, a tiny arena space particularly well suited to promenade production. The costuming was absolutely contemporary: suits for the conspirators, modern combat gear for the troops, and a posturing, medalled Caesar vaguely reminiscent of a Ceausescu or a Yeltsin. The actors moved through the space (sometimes with security guards clearing their path through the house) so that the audience was constantly moving to stay out of the way, get a better view or find a comfortable place to sit. When it came time for the forum scenes, the modern dress actors who moved among them were indistinguishable from those who had paid to come in, and the reduced scale of the whole made the orations feel like real conversations in which the audience were not just involved but implicated. The play felt like it was emerging from current conditions, current issues, current people, and the audience felt a level of engagement rare for this play.

An alternative strategy was pursued in Edward Hall's 2001 production at the Royal Shakespeare Theatre in Stratford, a production which married Thacker's approach with something like what Welles had done in 1937. This was an overtly political show which scrapped the first scene entirely and replaced it with a rousing song of the republic, a faintly soviet anthem about the love of the state trumping all other concerns. Normally the trimming of that first scene—in which the cobbler and carpenter banter with the outraged Flavius and Marullus—is a reduction of the ordinary people's importance to the play. The cobbler's punning is tricky for a modern audience to follow, but he shows an anarchically subversive wit, the cutting of which reduces the civilian population to the "blocks" Flavius believes them to be, making the show tacitly side with the aristocratic tribunes. Hall's cutting, however, allowed him to create a Rome in which dissent of any kind had already been subsumed by pervasive and omnipresent propaganda, the results of which accentuated the dangers of even thinking contrary to the official world view. There were no crowds of ordinary people in this production, only the party faithful, black shirted, jackbooted and wielding lengths of metal pipe. Welles had viewed the play as modelling the dangerous lure of Fascism; for Hall the state had long since succumbed to that lure.

Hall's funeral orations were thus given directly to the theatre audience, but that audience was also dotted with the menacing presence of the scripted crowd members. Instead of speaking for the theatre audience as their equals, however, these were *agents provocateurs*, thugs seeded among the masses to keep them in line. What the theatre audience felt, therefore, was not that (always tricky and potentially embarrassing) sense that the speakers around them were supposed to be articulating the audience's response to Brutus and Mark Antony, but the rather more alarming menace of silent coercion. The audience were not expected to join in the shouting or the ominous drumming on the railings with the metal truncheons the "crowd" carried; they were supposed to stay quiet and compliant, while more fanatical elements carried the day. This "crowd" were a citizen army which ground into action deliberately, not driven by the wild passion often seen in productions at the close of Mark Antony's funeral speech, but moved with robotic and meticulous callousness. When they stumbled upon Cinna the Poet, the only citizen other than the soothsayer who wasn't dressed like them, it was clear that they already considered him an undesirable intellectual. Caesar's assassination gave them the excuse to do what they had wanted to do before, so they cut out his heart and hung him upside down on stage. When Mark Antony entered for the following scene, he had to step around the corpse, but did so without giving it a second look.

Hall's production was not simply about creating political analogues echoing other places or points in history. In fact his *Caesar*, in setting itself outside a specific period or locale, did something which usually dulls the play's political edge by making it generic, but which, in its urgent performances and radical rethinking of the crowd, made a larger political statement about intellectual freedom. Indeed, the totalitarian state which the production presented was a study in the perils of a populace caught up in its own propaganda, incapable of generating real resistance at the level of ideas, and all too quick to see attempts to reform the system merely as the action of corrupt elements whose defeat would allow the restoration of all which had been threatened. Whether the old system ought to be reinstated was never seriously questioned, and from the moment of the assassination it was clear to this Brutus (wonderfully played by Greg Hicks) that he had made a terrible mistake and that his attempt to change the social system was doomed. When the "crowd" chanted in response to his funeral oration "let him be Caesar!", he realized that the people, or perhaps The Party, could imagine no other governmental structure. When he insisted that they let him depart *alone*, he knew he had already lost, and that Mark Antony would step into Caesar's shoes as the "crowd" clearly wanted.

In the same year as Hall's production, I worked as a dramaturg on a production of the play in Atlanta, Georgia. The director, John Dillon, set out to tell a distinctly southern version of the story, and the production was set in 1930s Louisiana, the title character modelled on that state's governor and presidential hopeful, Huey Long. Long, like Caesar, had a populist base, a dictatorial style verging on monomania and a similar end: he was shot to death on the steps of the Capital building in Baton Rouge in 1935. Taking the opposite tack to Hall, Dillon strove to make every aspect of the production evoke the place and period, anchoring the politics of the play in the kinds of detail its southern audience would find familiar and compelling. The murder of Cinna the poet after the funeral orations, was—as I said in the Introduction—the lynching of a young black man by a white mob. It was a risky choice that deliberately opened up wounds from Georgia's own non-too-distant past, though it did not play in the ways we had anticipated.

As referenced earlier, the intent to explore the recent past was derailed by the September 11 attacks on the Pentagon and Twin Towers which took place two weeks before the show opened. In the stunned days that followed, there were a series of reprisal attacks on Arab Americans which made national news, and it was these that many of the audience saw in our execution of Cinna the Poet. Productions are not always in control of their own political messages. I had feared that the lynching scene might be perceived as clumsy and overly deterministic, but contemporary association trumped everything the production had tried to do, though the result was, it might be said, more immediately relevant, more culturally apposite than the original directorial intent.

The attacks of September 11, 2001 reverberated through American politics for years after and led directly to the US invasion of Iraq, an act some leftist commentators saw as a cynical attempt on the part of George W. Bush to unite the nation under him and secure his second term as president in 2004. The war gave new specificity to political productions of *Julius Caesar*, one of which—directed by Deborah Warner at London's Barbican theatre in 2005—made direct association with the resultant combat in the Middle East, and with the political world which generated it. The troops wore contemporary desert combat fatigues while Anton Lesser's polished Brutus was generally regarded as a direct stand in for embattled British Prime Minister, Tony Blair. This was not the tortured liberal Welles had imagined in 1937, but a familiar contemporary politician of the New Labour stamp carefully— if misguidedly—trying to control the media "spin" of everything he did and said. Ralph Fiennes's Mark Anthony was a glamorous celebrity resembling David Beckham, who morphed from a sportsman at the Lupercal race in the second scene into a media-savvy politico at the play's midpoint. Almost everything in the production seemed to make a parallel between the ancient Roman and the contemporary British, though what it finally meant was less clear.

Some audiences and critics tried to treat the production as allegory, but for all the familiar resonances the modern situation did not clearly or easily match up with the play's narrative. Some found this confusing or took it to be a mark of failure, while others found the point less in the absence of a political statement about the war or New Labour, and more in one of the play's core reflections on miscalculation, on—as the play puts it—misconstruing everything. The play, like the British and American political situation, hinged on misreadings, on errors of judgement. Mark Antony's brandishing of Caesar's will and his bloody mantle, the visual aids he used to personalize his appeal that the crowd rise up and mutiny, were seen—like the legal documents presented by the clergy in the National Theatre's 2003 *Henry V* which I have already referenced—to echo the infamous "dodgy dossier" on weapons of mass destruction. The play's chaotic battles with their intimations of "friendly fire" disasters capped off a production less bent on establishing a political agenda and more with exposing the blundering, error-ridden chaos beneath the media spin of contemporary politics.

The election which secured Bush's second term as president was remarkably close and contested. Some critics felt that Bush defeated Democratic challenger John Kerry because of the involvement of conservative-leaning media corporations, particularly FOX news, who announced Bush's victory prematurely. When other networks followed suit—not wanting to be thought behind—polling (which was still going on) dropped off. The early announcement of victory became a self-fulfilling prophesy. This perspective on the election and global politics generally informed Falk Richter's 2007 German language production of *Julius Caesar* at the Burgtheater in Vienna.

The actors wore modern dress: slightly shabby suits suggesting a gritty, real world politics without the glamour one often sees in *Caesar*, the actors using a small, naturalistic style which prevented them from becoming over large or impressive. The upstage area was ringed with projection screens on which appeared key images (such as the statue of Caesar), but also the figure of a TV anchor woman, and a constant CNN-style news ticker. Richter's approach was, in a way, a more specific and technically sophisticated version of what Ron Daniels had done in 1983, but this later production was not simply trying to create an analogue between the play and modern media coverage of politics. This was a frontal assault on the manipulative power of politically and economically invested media empires, which outlast the individual emperors and presidents who seem to be in charge, feathering their own corporate nests. So the Brutus in this production assumed that the death of Caesar would lead to the deconstruction of the current state system and its media, while Mark Antony simply took Caesar's place. His funeral oration to the masses was a broadcast which combined Bush's post-9/11 demands for war with FOX news' cynical rabble rousing in his favour during the 2004 election.

This use of *Caesar* to explore ideas about contemporary mass media was expanded in the Toneelgroep's Dutch production which toured extensively from 2009 to 2012. The company combined *Caesar* with *Antony and Cleopatra* and *Coriolanus* into a six-hour production which took place as live action and continuous streamed projection all around the audience. That audience was encouraged to pay attention or not as the mood took them, the auditorium being arranged more as a lounge than a conventional theatre, with a bar and other deliberately ordinary distractions. Tickers flashed details of "historical" events and counted down to key moments such as Caesar's assassination. The production was intended to simulate the 24-hour news cycle which goes on around us, seeping into our consciousness and making us passively complicit in the careful narrative construction of world events.

I said above that political action routinely involving murder and factional war is not, mercifully, a version of the world in which most of us still live. But many people do, of course, and for them a play like *Caesar* is grimly apposite. Some recent productions, for instance, have drawn particular power from setting the production in contemporary Africa. Yael Farber's 2001 *SeZaR* played at the Grahamstown National festival of the Arts in South Africa and then toured regional theatres in the United Kingdom the following year. Farber combined Shakespeare's text with a mixture of Tswana translation, Pedi, Zulu, and contemporary English. This was a production expressly about Africa, albeit a generalized, Pan African imaginary state, particularly a nightmare of a postcolonial future in which African nations collapse in on themselves in a series of brutal tribal feuds. Traditional African folk dances were included, but so were news bulletins on the AIDS epidemic and other social crises. Cinna the poet was murdered in a painfully familiar "necklacing" (in which a burning tire is forced over the head of the victim), a device seen regularly in news footage from South Africa in the 1980s and 1990s. The war scenes mixed modern weapons with the machetes which figured in so many atrocities in Rwanda, and the stage was littered with brown limbs. Caesar himself was an amalgam of various African dictators and politicos: Chris Hani, Thabo Mbeki, Laurent Kabila, Robert Mugabe, Moise Tshombe, Patrice Lumumba, Idi Amin, and Jerry Rawlings (Wright 18). As Warner was to do four years later, Farber's production was less an argument about what was to be done and more a statement of what was, and its political edge was clearly as much about claiming ownership of the play as it was about unpacking possible African analogues from Shakespeare's text. In this, the decision to use multiple African languages is crucial, and is part of the reason I don't believe the production can be reduced to an image of the formerly colonized studying themselves through the colonizers' lens. Shakespeare gave Farber a myth and a platform, through and on which she was able to tell her own story. Like several of the other recent productions I have mentioned, productions such as Farber's treat the play as a vehicle for political meaning, rather than seeking to provide commentary on what seems intrinsic to the play as text. These stagings embrace the transformational and constructive power of theatre, making the script their own and finding ways to speak their own concerns through it.

The RSC's most recent production of *Julius Caesar* was also set in Africa, and featured an all black cast. A few elements of the show, directed by Greg Doran, might be familiar to those who had seen Farber's production (the necklacing, for instance) but the production's goals and methods were different. For one thing, this was not a heavily adaptive production as Farber's had been, but stuck closely to Shakespeare's script, and was widely praised for the elocutionary power and musicality which the cast were able to bring to the words with their African dialects. But the cast were actually home grown British actors, the production being the first at the RSC to sidestep colour-blind casting entirely and present an all black cast. The show found political specificity in its African setting, but its greatest political ramifications lay in what it meant for the future of the most visible Shakespeare company in the world to offer productions played entirely by minorities who have generally been marginalized by classical theatre.

Taken together, I think that what these productions demonstrate is the extent to which the inherent ambiguities of the Shakespearean text, its refusal to take absolute and unequivocal political positions, can be an asset for production, assuming that the goal is not simply to propagandize a univocal position. The plays can be made to speak to any number of issues, and even without rigorous adaptation can provocatively echo contemporary political debate even if the play itself does not provide simple answers. With more adaptation, of course, the production can more clearly advocate for a particular position, and in this non-anglophone productions have, perhaps, an advantage. Farber's *SeZar*, for instance, was less slavishly tied to the Shakespearean original by virtue of its translated script, something that renders old school complaints about cutting or changing the Bard's hallowed words moot, even as it makes the play a more malleable tool in the director's hands. For productions whose approach is less radical, the shows' politics are a matter of emphasis, of what gets underscored deliberately or (as in the post-9/11 Georgia Shakespeare production) what the audience thinks they are seeing. The contemporary political resonance of a play like *Julius Caesar* in no way attests to the play's timelessness, however; and the above examples show how hard productions have to work sometimes to prise contemporary relevance from its twice historically removed (Roman and Elizabethan) core, and I am, of course, excluding plenty of recent productions which were politically uninteresting. But in the hands of the right companies, with an eye for both larger issues and the detail of compelling performances, the play can be electrifying on stage and can seem, if not actually torn from the headlines, at least relevant to the political world in which the audience lives.

6
Place and Pedagogy: Site-Specific Production, School Tours, Prison Shakespeare, and the Question of Agenda

There is a deeply held cultural assumption that the performance of Shakespeare for (or by) those who are not customarily thought of as its audience—those in rural communities, say, but also the impoverished, the marginal, the young, and the incarcerated—is necessarily a Good Thing. Those audiences (or, indeed, players) are somehow uplifted by their encounter with the hallowed text, stunned by its apparent newness and "relevance," and transformed in ways benefiting society as whole.

What the supposed benefits of this proselytizing are, however, is harder to pinpoint, though there are more assumptions. In the case of young people, for instance, the Bardic encounter is supposed to help them excel in (or simply survive) school, while for prisoners that encounter gives them focus, constructive empowerment, and helps them get their lives together. Others are more generally elevated by their brush with serious or high culture, thereby partaking of what Pierre Bourdieu would call Shakespeare's "cultural capital," so that another familiar assumption emerges: the expansion of Shakespeare on stage, particularly for those less traditional audiences, is also a Good Thing.[1]

Jeremy Lopez has identified this latter assumption as what he calls the "missionary position" in most scholarly production reviews, a core component of which is the a priori belief that any staging of Shakespeare, however dull or incompetent, furthers the Shakespeare gospel (Lopez). Going out and teaching all nations (and subsets thereof) through live theatre is, apparently, sufficiently laudable, and productive an end that it gilds all manner of means.

We might call this the Bardeffect, that tendency of Shakespeare in performance to feel a little like going to church: something generally pretty dull which confers unspecific benefits on those who go and is thus treated with muted reverence. It is the Bardeffect which underlay the Bush Administration's support of the Shakespeare in American Communities project which I have already referenced (in Chapter 4), a large-scale NEA-funded initiative to tour Shakespeare productions all over the country, particularly communities that had little opportunity to experience live, professional theatre.

It is easy to be sceptical of such initiatives because of the flawed or politically wrong-headed notions which often drive them, but I want here to explore in more general terms the notion of Shakespeare staged outside traditional theatres, specifically in terms of their political ramifications. Are the consequences of such initiatives necessarily restrictive assertions of hegemonic values, or might there be something about location, the space of performance, and its attendant conditions, which is of value outside the Bardeffect?

In the Introduction, I explored the way theatre practitioners, such as Boal, attempted to subvert the monolithic cultural assumptions and audience disempowerment associated with traditional theatre through performance which takes place in unconventional spaces. Boal used a model of playmaking which generally did not depend on a pre-existing script, an option not open to companies intending to do conventional Shakespeare, but it is worth inquiring if the radical impulse of the non-traditional performance space can survive its facilitation of a traditional play, particularly one loaded with the kinds of cultural baggage which come with Shakespeare. In what follows, I want to consider both school and prison productions specifically as subsets of the site-specific or found space performance model.

In its broadest terms, site-specific performance merely suggests a production designed to play in a particular location as opposed to one which tours, but most practitioners use the term to imply a site which was not purpose-built as a theatre. Such usage brings the site-specific closer to the found space model, the difference only being whether the production can move to other locations. Some companies which use found spaces design their productions to be flexible enough to travel to other found spaces, but most assume that—as with site-specific productions—the nature of the performance space shapes the production in particular ways. To change the venue is to change the show.

Sometimes the decision to play in found spaces is a practical necessity for companies without the resources of their own theatre building, but many companies using this model say that the decision to use found spaces (say, rather than renting a theatre) is a deliberate choice which speaks to a particular notion of the kind of theatre they are making. PunchDrunk's production of *Sleep No More*, for instance, an adaptation of *Macbeth* staged in a series of derelict warehouses made to resemble an old-fashioned hotel, used the complex of "guest rooms" to create an interactive audience experience which thoroughly defamiliarized one of Western literature's most iconic texts. This is, I would argue, a political effect, one which renders the play new and immediate to a contemporary audience, though it does not of itself promote social change or even necessarily a conscious political sensibility. Other found space productions, however, use their locales to overt political effect.

Boston's Actors' Shakespeare Project, for instance, makes explicit the link between found space production and community engagement in its company mission statement:

> Actors' Shakespeare Project believes Shakespeare's words are urgently relevant to our times. Working as an ensemble of resident company members, we bring these words into the voices, bodies, and imaginations of our actors, audiences and neighborhoods. We do this through creative projects, including intimate productions and outreach programs that are informed by the spaces in which they happen. These projects inspire civic dialogue, build relationships between people, strengthen communities, and reveal something about what it means to be human here and now.
>
> ("Our Mission")

Abandoned warehouses, factories, swimming pools or hotels are selected for the way they resonate with the play to be staged, both in terms of the dynamics of their space and for their place in the local community. This is not merely a matter of physical properties (capacity, sight lines, and such) but associations which are rendered materially in the location. As such, the found space becomes as much about time as it is about place. As Kendra Fanconi of Vancouver's The Only Animal company puts it, "Place remembers," and in complex, suggestive ways:

> If it is a man-made location, say the old-time diner where Radix and I did the *Box* trilogy, it remembers the 1950s, but it also remembers that it is no longer the 1950s. A public pool, like the one in which the Electric Company and I made *The One that Got Away*, spans the elemental and man-made worlds: a pool remembers parties but it also knows drownings...The trees in Stanley Park, where boca del lupo

and I made *The Last Stand*, is a place that knows height in a way you and I never will. It is thinking backwards in time down to the ground. In a natural site, the memory is geographic. It remembers the beginning, when the Earth folded rock and the sea drowned valleys... I'm asking for these places to take me back in time, to the beginnings of stories that I was born in the midst of. (97)

Productions staged in such venues echo with the vestiges of what the place was, what it means to the people who know it. Because however derelict they might be, these places root the production in a version of both the past and the present, and as such they become a part of the community. Such spaces are aggressively local, they resist the impulse to universalize (the very impulse dogging many of those government mandated Shakespeare tours and vestigially present in the rhetoric about Shakespeare telling us what it is to be "human"), and the productions staged within them thus radiate a different species of engagement between the play and its audience. When chosen carefully, the venue speaks to something in the play which anchors it not in literary history but in the spaces in which people actually live.

To illustrate the point, I'd like to reference a production of *The Merchant of Venice* staged in Cork, Ireland, in 2005 by Corcadorca, a company resident in the city and characterized by "off-site" production and an international sensibility. This latter was particularly evident in the *Merchant of Venice* production which set out to tackle the comparatively new phenomenon of immigration—especially from Eastern Europe—into Ireland in general and Cork in particular. As Pat Kiernan, the production's director put it, "It seems appropriate to look at 'The Merchant of Venice' at a time when in Cork and Ireland we find ourselves suddenly exposed to different resident cultures and colours. How tolerant and welcoming are we?" (*The Merchant of Venice*). In order to foreground these issues, the production chose to see the play's exploration of anti-Semitism as a barometer of a more general otherness. As Lisa Fitzpatrick points out in her essay on the production, Cork's Jewish population is miniscule, so the director made the decision of having Shylock and the other Jews played by Polish actors who spoke with the kinds of strong accents that were becoming well known in the town, while a local Nigerian actor played Morocco (Fitzpatrick). The community represented by Antonio and Portia was aggressively xenophobic and racist.

That community extended beyond the professional cast, however, and this is where the site-specific nature of the production made its most telling and provocative collaboration. Cork, as a port city with busy river channels, docks, and warehouses, was a nice analogue of Venice, and the production exploited this connection by playing in promenade through the streets and at key locations in the city centre, notably a distillery, the court house (where the trial scene was played) and at a church where the production concluded. The audience—planted with extras—moved between these various venues, at one point marching on the court house brandishing banners with racist signs and calls for revenge against Shylock. Processions—religious and political—are a traditional feature of Irish life, and this one drew on the real to point up the political dimension of the production. It exposed the subsequent trial as a sham, but it also rendered the audience complicit, as did the jeering laughter at the accents of the "Jewish" characters. Since this procession moved through the city centre, the audience were themselves made performers for the casual bystanders.

As Fitzpatrick points out, the venues—particularly the church and the courthouse—were symbols of Irish culture and nationalism, albeit in vexed ways. Catholicism remains bound to Irish identity, though the present-day population is both less religiously homogenous and less devout than it once was, while the courts often stood for a justice system too closely allied with Britain for nationalist tastes, particularly over the treatment of IRA paramilitaries. The production thus probed and exploited tensions in the attitudes of the local populace to those institutions, while redirecting the focus onto the treatment of the immigrant and ethnically Other. The result was a palpable unease which drew extra potency from the peculiar intensity of shared experience which tends to dwell in promenade productions in which the audience members are more than usually aware of each other. Being active, moving en masse, and outside the privacy implied by the darkened auditorium of a conventional theatre, the audience are exposed to multiple stimuli from their surroundings. They see the action of the production (some of which was also shown in large-scale projection onto buildings), but they are free to look about them, to take in their (familiar) surroundings so that the material traces of their community become intertwined with the fiction which is being performed. Depending on their associations with those buildings and streets, the audience's sympathies may shift, perhaps empathizing with Shylock's predicament, or seeing the consequences of their own bigotry through a production which made central the service industry immigrants who were usually so marginal. As Fitzpatrick concludes, "This emphasis on shared presence facilitated the incorporation of the audience into the performance; and, through this experience of community, the production set out to create a new set of memories of the city and its streets" (183). What this kind of site-specific performance achieves then is analogous to Brecht's Epic theatre, in that instead of being entirely sucked into the fiction of the play, the audience is made self-conscious by their awareness of other audience members and by the setting which reminds them of their lives outside the play. This facilitates a kind of engagement which permits critical distance and self-awareness.

That it should be a play by Shakespeare which facilitated this event seems to me telling rather than paradoxical, since the point of the production was to rethink the cultural past. In this rethinking, an iconic play by one of England's most aggressively exported markers of cultural supremacy was appropriated for expressly Irish purposes. Such purposes were not, as might be expected, pointedly nationalist but sought to use the various dimensions of the past built into the fabric of the production as commentary on the present and an internationally diverse future which was mapped onto the very landscape of the town. The play is placed in dialogue with the community in which it is staged, shaped by the architecture of place and its curiously temporal rootedness. While production is often discussed in terms of its essential ephemerality, such a production becomes a part of the town's history, acting upon and building associative memory out of the fictive—the play—and the material—the locations as processed by the audience member.[2]

Audiences at site-specific productions like that in Cork are largely there voluntarily. School audiences, however, are largely not, and the politics of location thus factors differently, even oppositionally. In Chapter 7, I will discuss at length the idea of students staging Shakespeare in a university setting, but here I want to briefly consider the politics of Shakespeare productions which travel to primary, middle, and high schools. It is difficult to generalize about such things, of course, since each school and each travelling company is different, but it seems fair to say that touring productions are generally brought in as part of an educational strategy to make palatable a form of study which is expressly literary in focus. Performance is thus a kind of after thought, a method of chasing down those pedagogical holy grails: relevance to the students, engagement with the students, and ownership by the students.

The question of whether Shakespeare should be taught before college at all is beyond the scope of this book, though I am convinced that it should and that there is nothing intrinsically retrograde or conservative about doing so. How Shakespeare is taught is another matter entirely, and there seems to be little doubt that exposing students to the plays in performance tends to create a more dynamic form of engagement which—if done well—breaks down some student anxieties about the age and complexity of the language. If the burden of Shakespeare, that which makes his work potentially oppressive and disenfranchising, tends to inhere in its textual dimension, if it is in Shakespeare the Book that he feels most alien and elitist in the modern classroom, then it is in performance that more visceral and kinetic modes of reception and response take precedence in potentially liberating ways. Students who feel distanced from the letter of the printed, archaic page, intimidated or marginalized, generally feel much more comfortable responding to the bodies and voices of actors in ways which can build that sense of ownership even as the class leans back on the text to consider the choices made by the production they have seen.

Many professional companies have education departments and mount small cast productions designed to tour regional schools, and some universities (my own included) have similar programmes. Anecdotal evidence surrounding such productions, setting up and playing in high school auditoriums and gymnasiums, attests to the galvanizing effect of performing the plays on students who—in many cases—enter the event wary or hostile.[3] These shows tend to be stripped down for portability, so instead of relying on the kind of large-scale bells and whistles which can over determine audience response, they tend to rely on the interaction of the actors and their relationship with the audience. As with other forms of site-specific production, this dynamic foregrounds the larger environment–the audience as a community–and increases a sense of the play being done on the students' terms, even if their attitude to the school itself is ambivalent. I tour a lot of middle and high schools as both a Shakespearean and a novelist, and am always struck by the positive association audiences have with the sense of someone coming specifically *to them*, rather than the other way round. School is not home, but for most students it is still their turf, their realm, and this engenders a sense of comfort and belonging which might be disrupted by being ferried in buses to a traditional theatre.[4]

What the actual political consequences of touring productions are will depend, of course, on the nature of the production itself and how the school frames the event. Corcadorca's *Merchant* made politically inflected choices which gave resonance to their site-specific production without which the ideological valences of the show might have been radically different. Space/venue is obviously one of the shaping forces of a production's semiotics, but it cannot determine that production's political valences alone. But it is difficult to undervalue the consequences of a student watching actors make choices, responding viscerally to those choices and—hopefully—processing them intellectually after the fact. That those choices are being made *for* the student audience, as Boal knew, changes the place of the play in the hierarchical life of the student, shifting it from the tool of the establishment (the property of teachers, the subject of exams, the "cultural capital" which somehow connotes sophistication in later life) to a form of entertainment designed to engage. Many students enter such performances expecting to be bored, glad only of a break from conventional classes, and emerge transformed, not necessarily in love with what they have seen or suddenly convinced of its power to move, delight or teach, but—unshackled by the usual structures of the classroom—with opinions that feel immediate and defensible. Often they will see actors not so very different from themselves (something frequently confirmed in post-show talkbacks), people who have mastered this difficult material on their own terms without the legitimizing authority of being teachers. Shakespeare, say such productions, far from being something reducible to multiple choice testing, is there to be played with, to be explored, plundered for what you find interesting, for what speaks to you. For some students, this will amount to a form of ownership, and in so far as such feelings are empowering, is a political consequence of the production whatever the show's own specifics. Lastly, and perhaps most importantly, it should be said that productions which tour schools are—in many cases—the only form of live Shakespeare students are able to see, and in many parts of the United States, for instance, whose sheer size and cultural make up can mean that traditional theatres staging Shakespeare are well outside people's daily lives, they may be the only Shakespeare on stage those people will *ever* see.

I am focusing on audience response in schools because production *by* students is far less ubiquitous and is rarely compulsory. But if the politics of performing Shakespeare often hinge on ownership, then acting, as well as attending, is obviously a crucial way to break down the distancing effect of the text. Much has been written about the value and practicality of using performance in the classroom, and I will not add to it here, since the emphasis of such work is essentially rehearsal in nature and its aims are expressly pedagogical.[5] Suffice to say that actual wrestling with Shakespeare's text, putting it into one's own mouth, one's own body, is perhaps the surest way of breaking down its alien or oppressive associations. This is why staging Shakespeare has become something of a staple in another form of site-specific production, one which takes place in prison.

There is no greater instance of the way site-specific production brings performance to a population which might not otherwise see it than the programmes which mount Shakespeare productions in correctional institutions, nor is there a population whose demographic is less likely to be well versed in or well disposed to the plays' cultural heritage. In 1988, Jean Trounstine initiated such a programme at a women's prison in Framingham, Massachusetts, and published a detailed consideration of her work entitled *Shakespeare Behind Bars* in 2001.[6] Scholars such as Amy Scott Douglas have studied and written about programmes elsewhere,[7] and in 2005 a critically acclaimed documentary, also titled *Shakespeare Behind Bars* was released by Philomath films, directed by Hank Rogerson. In the Unites States alone, other programmes sprang up in San Quentin, Utah State Prison, Wabash Valley Correctional Institute, Racine Correctional Institute in Wisconsin, Riverfront State Prison in New Jersey and Suffolk County House of Corrections in Massachusetts, with similar developments in other English speaking countries.[8] In 2006, inmates of Maghaberry prison in Northern Ireland made a feature film adaptation of *Macbeth* called *Mickey B*.[9] In 2009, inmates of New York's notorious Sing Sing prison staged *Macbeth*, while the Kentucky-based programme which was the subject of the Philomath documentary continued to stage one major Shakespeare production each year, while also generating a new programme under the same name at the correctional facility in Muskegon Heights, Michigan.

The precise forms of these various programmes vary from institution to institution, but tend to be set up, managed and directed by theatre professionals working in close collaboration with the penal system and within the structures of prison culture. Scheduling restrictions mean that full productions take a long time to prepare (the Kentucky focused documentary suggests a rehearsal period of an astonishing 37 weeks), and cast members can be yanked from the programme for behavioural violations. Entire productions can be shut down by the warden if they seem to be aggravating rather than mitigating inmate volatility so that weeks or even months of shared work can be terminated without the performance that was their goal.

Such programmes do not see their mission as theatrical in aesthetic or pedagogically literal terms. Their goal is not for those involved to learn about the play but to treat the process of rehearsal and performance as a kind of psychosocial therapy, as the Shakespeare Behind Bars mission and vision statements written by the programme's founder Curt T. Tofteland make explicit:

Mission Statement

The Mission of Shakespeare Behind Bars is to offer theatrical encounters with personal and social issues to the incarcerated, allowing them to develop life skills that will ensure their successful reintegration into society.

Vision Statement

Shakespeare Behind Bars was founded on the beliefs that all human beings are inherently good, and that although convicted criminals have committed heinous crimes against other human beings, this inherent goodness still lives deep within them and must be called forth. Participation in the program can effectively change our world for the better by influencing one person at a time, awakening him or her to the power and the passion of the goodness that lives within all of us.

Shakespeare Behind Bars offers participants the ability to hope and the courage to act despite their fear and the odds against them. By immersing participants in the nine-month process of producing a Shakespeare play, Shakespeare Behind Bars uses the healing power of the arts, transforming inmate offenders from who they were when they committed their crimes, to who they are in the present moment, to who they wish to become.

("Mission & Vision")

These are, of course, lofty goals, and they contain assumptions about the arts in general and Shakespeare in particular that some will find difficult to swallow. As Scott Newstock, reviewing Amy Scott Douglas's book, points out, few academics would feel entirely comfortable subscribing to a version of theatre making which (according to the list of values which follows the vision statement) includes the development of a lifelong passion for learning, literacy skills, decision-making, empathy, trust, compassion, an increase in self-esteem, a sense of personal responsibility for crimes past, the peaceful resolution of conflict, the ability to work as a functioning member of a group and ultimately the capacity to rejoin society. This is a tall order to ask of inmates gathering together to perform Shakespeare.

And, predictably, not all involved benefit as the programme hopes. Some are unaffected by their time in rehearsal. Some, as Kirk Melnikoff suggests, may even find their Shakespearean roles bolstering some of their most antisocial, narcissistic or morally problematic behaviour, usually in ways that drive them from the programme. But there is no doubt that for some—most, even—the programmes achieve a lot which is good. The Shakespeare Behind Bars website boasts that while the national recidivism rate for prisoners is 67%, and that for Kentucky is 29.5%, the rate for members of the programme is only 5.4%. Such figures can be misleading, of course, because they may say as much about the temperament of the prisoners who are drawn to such a programme as they do about the programme's effects, and it may be that true assessment can only be performed at the level of individual cases.

But inmates in the juvenile programme attest that their involvement convinced them that they could do or be whatever they wanted in life. They call the experience a "life changer," something that has made them unrecognizable to those who knew them before. Wardens say that the programme showed them that with the right guidance, inmates really could change. One young participant said that standing as a member of the company at the end of a show gave him a feeling of exhilaration and belonging he had not felt since being incarcerated "Like I could fly or something." Others talk about learning to be themselves by playing other people or discovering what they can achieve without resorting to violence or illegal activity. They speak of the safety they feel in the programme, the sense of family and a resultant surety that they could control their own feelings, choices, and lives.[10]

It might be said, of course, that the testimony of individual prisoners to the transformative and redemptive power of their work with Shakespeare—and there is a lot of it, both in the documentary and in academic work which hinges on interviews with those involved—might not be entirely ingenuous. After all, prisoners' futures depend on parole board hearings where uttering the kind of pious or platitudinous statements that they might think those boards want to hear about how their theatre work has changed them may seem like a fast track to freedom, and—if nothing else—the programme has, presumably, made the inmates better actors. But such a view seems both unreasonably cynical and in defiance of a good deal of the evidence. Jean Trounstine's book ends with a series of sketches of the female prisoners she worked with on *The Merchant of Venice*, and all depict women who have left prison more confident, more in control of their lives, and have not reoffended. Statistics for the Kentucky juvenile programme for 2011 showed 94% improvement in class grades and 70% reduction in involvement in critical incidents, both of which point towards those remarkably low recidivism figures already cited. Summarizing, Hal

Cobb, who played Prospero in Tofteland's 2005 *Tempest* (the subject of the *SBB* documentary) says this:

> Being incarcerated often feels like being interred—dead to the world, dead to members of my family, dead to the church of my youth and former community. I imagine that if I am remembered, it is more likely for the evil I have done, eclipsing any good that may have occurred prior to or after that surrounds the commission of my crime. There is nothing inherent in a punitive justice system that requires me to look within myself or take personal responsibility. The ongoing work of Shakespeare Behind Bars facilitates the rare occasion of personal reflection to take responsibility for my personal choices, as well as providing an opportunity to remember and encourage my goodness. It doesn't ignore my shadow-self, but holds a mirror up to it, enabling me to embrace what I'd split from or hidden. The pursuit of character within SBB opens me up to aspects of my self (SELF) and embraces them in a holistic way.
>
> (Tofteland and Cobb 443)

Staging Shakespeare in prison clearly cannot reform a corrupt or ineffectual legal system, nor can it cure the ills of a society whose underclass are disproportionately likely to fall foul of that legal system. It cannot undo injustice or create a more equal world. But it can be a component in empowering the marginal, the people society has cast off as lost, and as such it can be a tool in transforming individuals, in facilitating a kind of self-transformation whose political value is no less significant for acting at the level of individual consciousness.

Whether these programmes would work less effectively doing plays by a different dramatist is another question. At the heart of their achievement is clearly a sense of shared labour and community which might transfer to other plays or kinds of activity, but regardless of what Shakespeare's language, stories, and characters "inherently" contain, the cultural vestiges of the Bard are not easy to substitute. Part of what makes Shakespeare work especially well in these different forms of site-specific production, and what reaffirms the unique power of these particular plays, is a combination of their cultural heritage (and baggage) paradoxically juxtaposed alongside their malleability: that curious sense that in spite of anxieties about historical authenticity most audiences are more willing to see updated or otherwise heavily adaptive productions of Shakespeare than they are of other playwrights. However much we know that *Hamlet* is the product of its Elizabethan cultural origins, audiences assume its capacity to move into an entirely different period setting in ways they rarely allow for more contemporary authors working in their own language. Authors whose work is performed in translation, Moliere, say, or the Greeks, seem to enjoy a similar contextual flexibility, though that is partly because the script is itself conspicuously mediated in ways Shakespeare generally isn't. When prisoners do Shakespeare they grapple with the thing itself, and the high cultural associations which are specific to Shakespeare are crucial for both the inmate's sense of individual mastery of that which is difficult and layered and for the programmes themselves which would probably not exist at all without such cultural associations to give them credibility. The Bardeffect is part of what gets these programmes into the prisons in the first place, and the fact that the assumption that Shakespeare is necessarily Good For Us is problematic doesn't mean that it can't be made to be true.[11] Again, the political value of staged Shakespeare derives not from the text or its monolithic cultural accumulations so much as from the theatrical product which is made through the particular investments and interactions of individuals in social (and physical) space. Scholars tend to be sceptical of the humanistic impulse to see Shakespeare as potentially transformative, particularly when positioned as a panacea for social ills, but I am just as sceptical of the notion that Shakespeare in prison is merely a kind of panopticon, in which the dispossessed are further pinned down and dehumanized by the weight of the Shakespearean cultural legacy. As Jean Trounstine remarked when one of her actresses new to the project said that Shakespeare was "white man's theatre": "Not," she said, "if we do it" (45).

7
The Tame Snake: The Politics of Safe Shakespeare

On the eve of the 2008 presidential election, United States president to be Barak Obama opted to give his final address before votes were cast from the campus of my present institution, the University of North Carolina at Charlotte (UNCC). The venue was not chosen idly. North Carolina was considered a key swing state, one which had traditionally voted Republican but which if it fell to Obama and the Democrats might model shifts to the left elsewhere in the country. Charlotte is the state's most major city (though not its capital) and UNCC is that city's major institute of higher education. As it happened, Obama won the election on the shoulders of states like North Carolina which did indeed vote Democrat. Four years later, after a bruising depression and the rise of the "Tea Party" Republican movement, the Democrats once more chose Charlotte, this time to play host to the Democratic National Convention where Obama would officially be named his party's nominee for the election which would follow two months later.

Charlotte has often been considered a blue (liberal) city in a red (conservative) state, and its recent time in the political spot light has hinged on this sense of it somehow representing a potential middle ground in what often seems to be a highly polarized nation. The city is a financial centre, a hub for Bank of America and Wachovia/Wells Fargo, and though it is not especially large (the population is about 1.8 million according to 2011 census data) it is still the only place in the state that feels like a major city, this despite the fact that the state government is located in Raleigh, three hours drive away. Much of the rest of the state is rural, white, relatively low income and conservative.

The university bills itself as the state system's urban research university, and though it leads the region in many areas, it still plays second fiddle in others, particularly to the flagship institution at Chapel Hill.

Most of our students lack the academic preparation necessary to attend top tier institutions, lack the funds to attend local power house private schools such as Davidson, Duke or Wake Forest, and are drawn to Charlotte as a city. Many come from rural areas and bring with them ties to forms of evangelical Christianity, a strong sense of family and conservative political assumptions both social and economic. At school, as is to be expected, many of them move away from these values, and many others don't have them to begin with, so the university, with its liberal-leaning faculty and urban environment, thus further emphasizes the sense of the campus as a liminal space in an otherwise birfuracted political landscape. While many campuses are assumed to be hotbeds of leftist activism, UNC Charlotte is politically more sedate, more cautious and, from a certain perspective, more balanced. Whether that makes its population more open to reasoned debate is arguable, of course, but it does seem plausible to say that the university's social and geographical position makes it a barometer of the wider political climate and therefore, as its primacy for the National Democratic Party and the Obama administration makes clear, a highly contested space. Winning over hearts and minds here has larger repercussions for a deeply divided nation.

It was in this highly charged atmosphere that I directed *A Midsummer Night's Dream* in the spring of 2010, in a purpose-built outdoor location in one of the campus green spaces close to the main theatre building. The production was part of an initiative called "36-in-6" managed by the school's Shakespeare In Action initative to mount some form of public event connected to each Shakespeare play in the six years leading up to the 400th anniversary of his death in April 2016, though the funding and logistical arrangement was done through the university's theatre department in which I am a faculty member.

The department's support for the 36-in-6 project amounted to a commitment to stage one Shakespeare play per year as part of its five-show annual season, the choice of play being heavily inflected by what would seem to be a draw for audiences. Times were hard and the department, which had recently gone through some significant administrative changes, including being moved into a new college, was keen to attract attention to its work, both as a way of building its box office takings to underwrite future productions and student scholarships, and more generally to be seen contributing to the life and reputation of the university. The decision to stage *Dream*, and to do so outdoors, arose at least in part due to such concerns. This was, it was assumed, a crowd-pleaser, a light, fun romp of a play well suited to an outdoor venue. The rhetoric accompanying the initial discussion of the show—and the wholly positive reactions we received from people on and off campus when we discussed what we planned—assumed that this would be a charming production and, not to put too fine a point on it, a safe one.

Anyone who has read any literary criticism of this play from the last half century will know that such a reading is far from a given. The play is potentially rife with real conflict, with struggles over gendered power, with issues of forced marriage, manipulation, desire, sexuality, class warfare, and a host of potentially provocative and challenging issues. But *A Midsummer Night's Dream* has a curious place in the popular consciousness and the overall impression, one which has survived several decades of new classroom approaches, edgy theatrical stagings and the occasional fairly sexy movie, is that the play is largely fluff. This seems to come from the pairing of a love story which resolves (it is assumed) happily, with the playful antics of some lovable fairies, an absence of extensive bawdy and no actualized violence. The result is Shakespeare as tame snake: interesting, pretty, a little odd, but child-friendly and ultimately fangless.

I had no interest in such a production, but the valence of safety did present an opportunity to engage an audience which, as I have already said, was likely to be politically fairly conservative but not rootedly so, in a consideration of ideas which would emerge from the play but which would also be *about* the play and the place of Shakespeare generally, while also touching on issues far from resolved in our community: race and gender roles, for instance, sexual orientation, familial authority and more general ideas about self-fashioning, personal discovery and change. This was never to be a manifesto or a browbeating of the audience. It was not a radically new approach to the play, nor was it supposed to be politically incendiary. Rather it was to use those assumed elements of playfulness, of safeness, to push a little beyond the collective comfort zone in ways which would create not outrage, but—hopefully—real thought. The intent was to be subversive, but carefully so, using a softly-softly approach that was nuanced and engaging so that the audience would not retreat behind ideological barriers.

A Midsummer Night's Dream presents the opportunity to explore a key cultural clash between the Athenian court and Theseus in particular, and Hippolyta, the Amazon queen whom he has taken in battle and will finally wed. I had opted to read the play in terms of the inherent tension of this forced marriage (one echoed by that facing Hermia at the end of the first scene) but wanted to get to an ending which would feel genuinely festive, not tragic, one which would engage the audience rather than alienating them. In order to do this, the core production team decided early on to use the familiar doubling of Theseus/Oberon, Hippolyta/Titania so that the tensions of the first scenes could be worked out through the human characters' fairy alter egos before the nuptial celebrations at the end. My Theseus, Demetrius and Helena were white, while Hippolyta and Lysander were black. Hermia was Latina, but her father, Egeus, was white. In each case (including the last, in which we had to imagine a now absent Latina wife for Egeus), the casting was to be played not as colour blind, but with the race of each character being allowed to signify.

Allow me to place the issue of race in local and historical context. Like most southern states, racial unrest marked the Jim Crow period through to the civil rights era of the 1960s throughout North Carolina, and though these struggles lacked the worst of the violence experienced in places like Alabama and Mississippi, Police and National Guardsmen killed a student demonstrator in Greensboro (where the influential Woolworths sit-in occurred in 1960) as late as 1969. Ten years later, the state ended the eugenics programme which, since 1929, had ordered the forcible sterilization of nearly 8000 "feeble-minded" people, mostly poor and black. The debate over reparations for the eugenics programme raged throughout 2011 and was resolved in early 2012 with the decision to donate $50,000 to each of the 1500–2000 survivors of the programme. Activists argued that the final amount was insufficient, while opponents of the pay out claimed that the impoverished state budget should not be made to bow to minority interests over what was essentially ancient history. That sense that race relations are a matter of the distant past is a familiar one in the south, one that ghosts my more conservative students' assumptions about success being bound to individual work ethic and talent, rather than the material conditions and cultural environment into which one is born. They know such things have to be voiced carefully and with various caveats attached, but there is no question that some of our students feel some resentment over what they perceive to be a privileging of black history and issues on campus. Discussing African American plays such as George C. Wolfe's *The Colored Museum* in class (it was one of our spring 2012 productions) creates a palpable unease in which some—not all by any means—of the white students feel unqualified to speak to the play's subject matter, some going so far as to wonder why they are being asked to read a play which does not—they think—have any relevance for them. While some students profess a "post-racial" attitude and seem quite comfortable with groups of friends which seem to ignore racial lines, there is a hesitancy to discuss the region's racial past and a reluctance to accept (in the face of all manner of evidence) that that past continues to influence the present. Race relations are frequently treated as a moral concern which has already been vanquished rather than an economic one, and the very separateness of black cultural identity is thus seen as wilfully divisive, something which should be jettisoned in favour of more complete assimilation into the dominant (white) hegemony.

Partly as a result there was an element of muted shock among our diverse cast when we first began to discuss the racial dynamics of the show, something they had clearly not expected. Indeed, after some preliminary conversations it seemed to me that the racial component did not require significant investment from the actors in terms of back story or motivation (ours was a largely realist show with a fairly naturalized sense of character psychology), relying rather on the simple fact of their various ethnicities acting upon the awareness of the audience. Hippolyta wore the faintly Edwardian garb of the Athenian court, but instead of the muted creams of the other ladies, hers were in bold and colourful African prints, and when she shed much of it to be Titania, her corset was decorated by bead-like shells. Lysander under the spell of the love juice took to throbbing to a music only he could hear, punctuating his lines with the glib gestural vocabulary of black R&B boy bands. Moreover, not focusing on the psychology of race in rehearsal in no way lessened the impact of seeing it in the show: Egeus's fury over his daughter's choice of Lysander suddenly looked a lot like Brabantio bewailing Desdemona's marriage to Othello, a resonance which gave special weight to his charge that Lysander had somehow bewitched his daughter. When the lovers were discovered in Act IV, Hermia's attempt to reconcile with her father was brushed off, and Egeus did not appear in the final scene at all. His was an enactment of the lingering effects of that "ancient history" still felt—if usually left unarticulated—in the American south where interracial relationships are concerned.

That the production finally celebrated such relationships (in the marriages of both Hermia/Lysander and Theseus/Hippolyta) might have gone for little, the sense that we were fighting a battle which was long won, except that we were warned by a cast member to expect a disruption to the show during a particular performance. Apparently members of the actor's family would be in attendance, and she fully expected them to stage some form of protest about the representation of interracial relationships. The police were notified before the show and made their presence felt around the auditorium. Whether as a result or not, no such disruption occurred. But while I would like to take this as a sign that the matter of interracial relationship really is a dead issue in North Carolina, the evidence provided by the Southern Poverty Law Centre is less encouraging. Their website, which tracks hate groups and their activities indicates that in November of 2011, seven black churches in Ansonville, NC, were daubed with swastikas and racial epithets, and similar incidents of racially motivated graffiti appeared in Winston Salem, Greensboro and Hayesville earlier in the year. Moreover, the SPLC identifies 28 hate groups in North Carolina, mainly Ku Klux Klan, white supremacist and neo-Nazi. Tellingly, perhaps, the only one officially located specifically in Charlotte is a black separatist group, the Nation of Islam.

It is one of the peculiarities of campus productions that their audiences are often stacked with friends and family of the company members, many of whom have travelled from outside the city—and therefore from quite different cultural environments—in order to see the show. I cannot speculate on the effect our production had on such people, but I feel confident saying that however non-confrontational we thought the handling of race, there would be some in the audience who felt otherwise, even if they did not express their feelings. The production took a political side and celebrated it, and if that position seems old hat, it is worth remembering that theatrical meaning finally lies in the minds of the audience, and for some of ours, the sight of a white Oberon kneeling in supplication to his black spouse, was anything but "safe."

That moment of supplication came out of the production's preoccupation with the specifically gendered power struggles in the play. As in the final scene of *The Taming of the Shrew*, the manner of Oberon's victory over his headstrong wife can be extremely troubling, his use of the love potion to humiliate her into falling in love with the monstrous Bottom a breaking of female power, voice and will in a celebration of patriarchy. Whether this is the best reading of the text or the way a Renaissance audience may have understood the play's conclusion did not finally concern us unduly. Our production was of and for the present and we had no interest in perpetuating a misogynist version of the story. We were, however, determined to use the play text with only minor editorial trimming, so we had to think through the logic of the Oberon/Titania power struggle in ways which would facilitate a happy ending for both of them and for the audience, particularly since the end of their wrangling was what (in our doubled production) would also unify Theseus and Hippolyta.

The show opened with Hippolyta performing a sword exercise, mimicked by the Indian (or Changeling) boy whom we added throughout the production—a son (biological or adopted, we did not say, though the child actor was mixed race—white and Asian) for the Amazon Queen, an adopted fairy page for Titania. When Theseus entered he was clearly displeased by both the sword exercise and the Queen's dalliance with the boy, both of which he saw as remnants of a life and an independence he wanted her to give over. She resisted his cajoling into a simple celebration of their upcoming nuptials and, on seeing him take Egeus' side over Hermia's marriage, ignored his desire to leave with him, storming off and into what would be the fairy forest with the boy. The silent fury felt by Theseus and Hippolita became fully vocal in the fairy world, where both actors reappeared, their costumes slightly modified, their physical styles more clearly bestial and closer to the ground in the "Ill met by moonlight" scene.

The production, for all its physical stylization and expressly theatrical use of our outdoor setting, was—broadly speaking—psychologically realist, so figuring out how the Oberon/Titania conflict resolved required more than a political overlay. As I have said, we wanted a happy ending and that meant that Titania/Hippolita could not be broken and humiliated at the end, nor—worse—could she be unaware of how deeply she had been manipulated. I didn't want their reconciliation to be Oberon's smug wink at the audience, so we had to determine how to process the dynamic in ways that would allow us to make a point about equality while staying true to both the internal logic of the play and the sense of these characters as thinking, feeling people, not symbols. We began to play with the idea that, contrary to initial assumptions and the explanation he gives to Puck before removing the charm from Titania's eyes, Oberon does not actually win. Rather, his plan backfires. Titania is perfectly happy with the half-transformed Bottom, feeling (in her magically drugged state) no shame in the match at all, while Oberon is gripped both by a sense of the sexual jealousy he expressed in Act II Scene I and, more poignantly, by a sense of loss: the spell makes him irrelevant to her. On stage this was manifested by his finding her entwined around Bottom and ignoring the Indian boy who had been all her focus earlier on. The tableau showed him and the audience the extent to which she had been changed, her new single-mindedness revealing how much of her had been stripped away. Oberon was then made to realize that what he wanted was not dominance over her, but for her to have the will to choose him, though he knew that that would also bring with it her old self-possession and defiance.

In short, he realized that what he had loved was the whole, potent person of Titania, and that his apparent victory was, in fact, a defeat. He saw in the abandoned Indian boy an image of himself, alone and irrelevant, and knew that his own happiness was dependent on her capacity for self-determination. His words to Puck were thus a kind of blind which neither of them believed, and the spell which revived her—"be as thou wast wont to be"—was a telling capitulation. His embrace of the Indian boy then showed how he would no longer attempt to exclude her past, and when she revived, he responded to her wary questions about how she came to be here with Bottom, with the aforementioned supplicatory kneeling. This last came late to the rehearsal period and became (for me) a moment which was both touching and potent, as he laid down the authority he had clung to and she, knowingly, lovingly, raised him up again as she had formerly raised the kneeling, weeping Hermia when she had been brushed aside by Theseus, her father and Athens' patriarchal law. The point was political, but presented in terms of individual choices within a couple's relationship, and it resonated across the other couples in the play so that Helena's waking realization that she had found Demetrius "like a jewel, mine own and not mine own" became a mantra for the cast: love is not about possession or ownership, but is grounded in mutual respect and self-determination.

This is a familiar idea, but in the context of older notions of love such as are assumed to be central to Shakespeare, it is an important one, and a mark of how the play was being rediscovered, remade by the community which generated the production. In the curiously liminal space which is our campus, a place and a community on the cusp of various social and political impulses, a formative environment for our students positioned distinctly in the middle of the nation's polarized political landscape, this was—I think—a thoughtful production, one which wrestled with real issues both personal and schematic in good faith. I doubt many of those who saw it felt politically browbeaten by the race and gender issues, but I do think their responses, however muted, however minor and taken for other things, were political. Sometimes political productions which operate under the ideological radar achieve more and reach a wider range of audience than do those whose methodologies are more shrilly agitprop, even if what they actually say is less controversial or confrontational so much as it is a declaration of what we take now to be culturally and therefore politically normal.

A Midsummer Night's Dream foregrounds class concerns in the gap between the lovers/courtiers and the "rude" mechanicals. Our production emphasized this gap first through costuming. Instead of the elegant dresses of the ladies and faintly Prussian formality of the men's uniforms, our mechanicals were a cross-section of servants and manual labourers, easily recognizable by the tools of their trade. Flute (played by a woman) was a miner, Starveling a factory worker, Snug a welder (whose mask became the basis of his lion head), Bottom, a construction worker, Quince (also a woman) a lady's maid and Snout (an African American woman) a street vendor. Though we assumed Bottom was known from other acting work, the mechanicals did not know each other when they first met, so Quince's role call was no formality. They were initially wary of each other, particularly Flute who was aggressively surly, and their journey through the production was one of finding a shared identity rooted in common goals. At the end of their play within the play, they were all given checks which were, based on their responses, for vast sums of money, producing not just laughter but also shock, even tears. That the money was dolled out so casually by Theseus's servant poignantly underscored the difference between the two classes. But the mechanicals' journey was not simply to relative wealth. Rather it was to a sense of community which they built with their own artistic labour, forming bonds of friendship and love which gave them a new sense of purpose and identity. Their initial separateness, even hostility, was transformed through the shared embarrassments of rehearsal, the terror of what happened to Bottom in the forest, their depression when all seemed lost, their delight when Bottom returned and their sense of triumph over their slightly hostile audience in the final performance. Crucially, that final performance, despite their palpable fear of reprisals, permitted a sense of group identity which morphed into a class-based defiance. They stood up for themselves when heckled, insisted that they be taken seriously, and when Bottom corrected Theseus's reading of the play's action (over whether or not the wall should speak again), he did so not as the company's star, someone the others simply idolized, but as their mouthpiece and friend. When the courtiers joined the mechanicals in the final bergomask it was to acknowledge their achievement and to accept a form of equality with them, though it was the bonds between the mechanicals themselves that were paramount. By the end of Pyramus and Thisbe, Bottom and Flute were a couple, Starveling's homosexual interest in Bottom had turned to reciprocated friendship and the whole group had become a mutually supportive unit which did not need the praise of the courtiers to validate their work.

This sense of an underclass coming together through work was a motif for the company itself, an unlikely group wrestling with one of the great figures of literature and theatrical tradition and trying to find a way to own it. This struggle was deliberately extended beyond the company itself to include the audience, something aided by the daylit outdoor space, and the fact that audiences were asked to move twice (from Athens to the woods and back), led by the mechanicals. From the earliest stages of rehearsals the actors were encouraged to use direct address wherever possible, to make eye contact with the audience and draw them into the action, sharing it and embracing the idea that they were collaborators in the show's generation of meaning. The script was dotted with adlibs, with moments where the performers consulted with the audience (as when, for instance, Helena sought someone to help repair her increasingly shredded dress), with looks and gestures designed to extend the sense of community to those watching, to make the whole—in spite of its antique script—feel as close to spontaneous action as possible. It was, I like to think, the kind of production whose empowering inclusiveness might have pleased Boal, and whose use of a quasi Elizabethan, non-realist theatrical dynamic (even though the acting itself was broadly realistic and psychologized) might have pleased Brecht. The exuberance of the final dance to music improvised by the cast emphasized a sense of ownership which made manifest the logic of the daylit space and said that this was a communal and connective experience.

I have little more than the audience's applause to suggest that the strategy was successful, and even less to ground a sense of the production's political effect. What was clear, however, was that for the company, its friends, families, and the others who populated our audience over the show's sold out two-week run, something was achieved which made the play edgier than expected but also somehow unmistakeably ours.

And the audience's. The show played to the particular community which is our campus, bolstered by the friends and family of those involved but—with the exception of a couple of matinees for local schools—almost completely devoid of people from the surrounding area who had no prior ties to the school. This, like many site-specific productions, was a show of and for our immediate population. If inmate testimonials of the effects of prison Shakespeare have to be taken with a grain of salt, students enthusing about their experience to their professor and director probably require still more seasoning, but Leslie Gray, an African American junior who played Snout, identified something I thought telling because I don't recall it ever being directed. Our mechanicals began very much as individuals, entering separately, standing awkwardly, silently apart till Bottom's (late) arrival gave Quince the cue to draw them all together. Snout was the only black character in the scene and kept herself embarrassedly apart. The only character to acknowledge her presence was Tyler Waddell's gay Starveling, who was to fall in love with Bottom as the production progressed. This was a choice which emerged from rehearsal rather than being determined from the outset, and it evolved out of the simple factor that the actor himself was gay, and in messing about in rehearsal had stumbled onto a rich and funny sense of his character and that character's relationships with the others. For Leslie, there was a verisimilitude in the immediate connection of the mechanical company's only gay man and its only black woman since "even in small groups, minorities tend to seek each other out and stick together" (Gray). For at least some of the cast, then, the radicalism of the production hinged on allowing their sense of who they were as subjects to engage actively with the play. The political consequences were not determined by the play alone, but by their engagement with it, an engagement which broke down assumptions about what Shakespeare was and who it was for. As Leslie said:

> I think Shakespeare productions have always been one of those things that I have always thought of as being non-negotiable, white washed plays. I am not really sure what drove me to audition for the show; I was not at all prepared for the result. From the first table reading after casting, it was made clear that race and gender were apparent and real issues that would be represented and addressed within the play. I think, as a black female, it is incredibly frustrating to be constantly cast in roles that do not acknowledge the fact that I obviously don't fit into the preconceived notion of those roles. I initially thought that there was nothing in the play that spoke to any of the mechanicals being cast as diverse in terms of either race or gender. However, through the constant exploration into how they work within the realm of greater society, we were able to find an identity within the characters that recognized the harmony of being social outcasts in both theatre and the real world. In the end, the audience was better suited to empathize with this goofy bunch of non-actors getting onstage because during the course of the play, we were able to show a struggle past race and sexuality which is the reality for many of the cast members as well as the audience viewing. The gravity of the situations and humanity of each character is what gives the comedic play relevance and allows it to resonate today.

The politics of a production are finally about what those engaged in it—audience and company—think and feel about their experience and the way it negotiates cultural value, including their own. For most students in the twenty-first century, Shakespeare is Other, something whose value has been constructed by people and social structures from which they feel largely separate. One form of political activism would be to simply toss Shakespeare out as irrelevant. Another, and one which keeps the baby while changing the bathwater, is finding a way to deconstruct that Otherness, not through teaching its universal applicability, its transhistorical, transcultural genius, but by acknowledging the present, the geographical and temporal space of the production, its means of construction and transmission and the other material conditions which surround it as equally valid co-creators of meaning as is the hallowed text. Preeminent among those conditions are the people who build the production, those who act it, who watch it, whose consciousness and experience shape the theatrical event and own it. This is how we break down the Bardeffect, how we make the plays speak our concerns, our issues, our identities and how—politically speaking—we rescue Shakespeare from his own legacy.

Part III
Provocation and Debate

8
"A Conversation with Ayanna Thompson in Three Acts"

Act 1: Context is all

Andrew, you rightly warn that in all matters of political theatre, "Context, here, is all." Keeping this mantra in my mind, I begin with a very specific example of political theatre, the Eden Troupe at Patrick Henry College (PHC).

Founded in 2000 by Michael Farris (who now operates as its Chancellor), Patrick Henry College defines its mission as "preparing Christian men and women who will lead our nation and shape our culture with timeless biblical values and fidelity to the spirit of the American founding."[1] When PHC opened its doors, Farris specifically targeted evangelical Christians who were homeschooled and who desired not only an "authentic Christian environment" but also "preparation for 'careers of influence' in politics."[2] The first two years of the PHC curriculum are based on a type of liberal arts, Western Civilization, great thinkers/books model, but the final two years are based on a "vocational model" in which students receive credit for internships and research projects.[3] The cultivation of students at PHC, then, is premised on the notion that this generation of Christians has to be actively involved in politics. Farris argues that internships in Washington, DC are central to the development and success of the students because, "A whole lot of elected members of Congress started off as Hill staffers. If you want to train a new generation of leaders, you have to get in on the ground floor."[4] In its first five years in existence, PHC students won roughly the same amount of internships in the White House as did students from the more politically entrenched Georgetown University (established 1789). Politics are at the heart of PHC.

Fascinatingly (but perhaps not surprisingly), PHC's first, and now oldest, student-run organization is a theatre troupe called the Eden Troupe, which has put on many different full-scale productions of Shakespeare, including *As You Like It, Much Ado about Nothing, Macbeth, Twelfth Night,* and *Midsummer Night's Dream.* In a publicity piece released on March 31, 2012, Sarah Pride makes it clear that directing a production for the drama club is defined as a significant leadership role at PHC: "The role of Eden Troupe director is one of the largest leadership tasks a student can undertake at PHC."[5] While organizing the complex logistics of a theatrical production clearly requires leadership skills, leading the Eden Troupe also requires political skills. On the club's website, for instance, the Eden Troupe is defined as "a student arts organization that seeks to glorify God through the production of plays that communicate truth and beauty."[6] Likewise, the drama club is identified as providing an important outreach service to the community: "Eden Troupe is one of the College's best-known community outreaches, bringing in audience members from the local area and occasionally local members of the press."[7] And moreover, student actors and directors often define their work in religio-political terms, as exemplified in these statements in another press release:

> "Drama represents truth in a way that connects with people," [Stephanie] McGill says. "Christians can produce any kind of play in a way that illustrates truths we all need to know." [Aidan] Grano agrees about the great potential of Christian drama. As he puts it, "Drama lets us step out of our daily lives and observe the truth and falsehood of the same choices we make, acted out in others' lives. In judging them, we judge ourselves. Also, it is a fun activity that allows us to exercise our God-given creativity."[8]

The Eden Troupe's mission, then, is political theatre: to illustrate Christian truths.

The troupe's 2005 production of *Macbeth* exemplifies PHC's approach to political theatre. In their director's note for the production, Maggie Dougher and Carolyn Thomson locate their concept for the play in the intersection and clash of not only paganism and Christianity but also evil and redemption:

> Welcome to old Scotland, a dark country in which good and evil are fought out by spiritual choices and strong swords. Christianity has only recently penetrated with the conversion of King Duncan and his family.... Bitter because the people no longer worship them, the witches embody the influence of sin, enticing mortals and rejoicing

in their destruction. Yet Macbeth reminds us how impotent evil is. In chasing after lawless ambition, Macbeth and Lady Macbeth catch emptiness and insanity.... Evil is a mere apparition, a knocking, three witches who can suggest but not perform without permission from a mortal's will. In Scotland, as in our world, when the rightful King resists, evil must flee.[9]

PHC's approach to drama, then, is to communicate and spread a Christian worldview because, as April Wright an alumna of PHC testifies, "Drama is such a powerful medium for communication."[10]

How does this example of political (by way of evangelical) Shakespeare fit into your vision of political theatre? The rhetoric employed by the Eden Troupe members is not far from the rhetoric you cite from Bertolt Brecht, Peter Sellars, Peter Brook, and other left-leaning directors. The PHC students, after all, recognize the flexibility of Shakespeare's plays and the imperative to create politically charged productions (e.g. "Same script, same characters, but completely different message")[11]; as such, they create specific contexts for their productions (e.g. ancient-pagan Scotland for *Macbeth* and contemporary New York City for their 2009 production of *Twelfth Night*)[12], and they have a clearly articulated political agenda (e.g. "to glorify God through the production of plays that communicate truth and beauty").[13] While you occasionally acknowledge that not all political theatre will be liberal or left-leaning, more often you associate intentionally constructed political theatre with liberalism and "traditional" theatre with conservatism. As the Eden Troupe exemplifies, however, there are also intentionally constructed, conservative political productions, and one does not have to imagine the most far-right extreme example (e.g. the Nazi's use of *Merchant of Venice*) to frame intentionally constructed, politically conservative theatre. There are the Eden Troupes, the Movers and Shakespeares (Ken Adelman's programme for businessmen), and various other conservatively motivated organizations that employ Shakespeare strategically and politically.

Academics are often chided by conservatives for being leftist in our political views and approaches to education, and I think Shakespeareans might fall under that critique as well. While there is a lot of scholarship about the conservative underpinnings to and assumptions about Shakespeare's cultural capital, Shakespeareans have not fully acknowledged, addressed, and analysed what I would call the intentionally constructed, politically conservative Shakespeares. Thus, I am left wondering if every type and stripe of political theatre is the same in your estimation. Are all political Shakespeares good and/or socially beneficial? Or, am I asking the wrong question academically, theatrically, and/or politically?

If I may be permitted to focus on the production side for a little while longer before turning our conversation to reception, I wonder how your practical assessment of and guidance for political theatre fits with or against Robert Brustein's views about conceptual directing. You advise that political Shakespeares are most effective and powerful when they are context specific. No one production, you sagely intone, will have the same political valences in different locations and times: "Context, here, is all." Therefore, directors need to have very clear and targeted concepts for the specifics of their company, audience, neighbourhood, historical moment, local political history, and so forth.

Robert Brustein has defined this type of approach as "conceptual directing," and he breaks conceptual directing into two different forms: "one that depends largely on external physical changes and another that changes our whole notion of the play."[14] Through an analogy that employs figures of speech, Brustein links these two forms with "the prosaic simile and the poetic metaphor": "The simile approach is more familiar, at least to New Yorkers, because it is often used by visiting British companies and over the years in Joseph Papp's Shakespeare productions.... All these productions were known inside the trade as 'jollying Shakespeare up.' "[15] Metaphorical directing, Brustein reveals, is more European in approach: "Updating is a shorthand way of showing how the material of a classical play has topical meaning for contemporary audiences. And when directors use this approach for thematic rather than ornamental purposes, it can be valuable and illuminating."[16]

As many will remember, Brustein is a staunch advocate for colour-blind casting because he believes that Americans should be able to move beyond race. In fact, he debated fiercely with the black playwright August Wilson (both in print and in person) about the role of racial casting in contemporary American theatre (Wilson was against colour-blind casting because he saw casting actors of colour in classical plays as "deny[ing] us our humanity, our own history, and the need to make our own investigations from the cultural ground on which we stand as black Americans"[17]). While many scholars have written about these debates, no one has tied Brustein's stance on colour-blind casting to his interpretation of conceptual directing. For Brustein, directors like Joseph Papp and Orson Welles, who relocate Shakespearean plays to different locations so that they can employ non-white actors, are the lesser simile directors (e.g. Welles's so-called Voodoo *Macbeth* production with an all-black cast at the Lafayette Theatre in Harlem in 1936). Brustein argues that these productions are "rarely more than a novelty of surfaces, skin-deep, and marred by traces of voguishness."[18]

Brustein identifies the more highly valued metaphor director, on the other hand, as one who moves beyond the ornamental to the thematic, and he specifically cites Bertolt Brecht, Peter Brook, and Ingmar Bergman as directors who create metaphorical productions of Shakespeare. With the exception of Brook, however, these directors rarely, if ever, worked with actors of colour. (It is also worth noting that Brustein specifically praises Brook for his 1970 RSC production of *Midsummer Night's Dream*, which did not employ a racially diverse cast, rather than his later work with the International Centre for Theatre Research which employed a multinational, multiracial, and multilingual cast.)

Is there a way, then, to discuss metaphorical directing and racial casting? Do you agree with Brustein's analysis of conceptual directing (with the simile directors and the metaphorical directors)? Are these terms and concepts useful for your approach to political theatre? If you do not find them useful, where exactly do you part ways? And if you do find them useful, what can you add to Brustein's analysis? For example, while you also look to Brecht and Brook when you discuss political theatre, you do not look to them when you address identity politics in performance. Is there a way to make their approaches and examples work within the larger context of our multicultural world? Or, do we need to look to other theories, examples, and models to be able to do so? While you very compellingly demonstrate how casting with regards to race, gender, and sexuality is a political act, you do not tie those artistic/political decisions with the larger debates in political theatre.

Act 2: Reception is all

It is important to shift focus to reception, however, because the bulk of your book brilliantly foregrounds the ways that "Reception is all." As you remind us, the meaning(s) of any given political Shakespeare production will accrue over time in ways that may not be anticipated by the producers, directors, actors, critics, or audiences. The "political effect is created in the minds of the audience and is therefore plural, contradictory and irreducible" regardless of what the theatrical company says its political intentions are (or are not). While I could not agree more with this argument, I am still puzzled about what to do with the complex and dynamic implications it has for the study of political theatres' audiences.

First is the puzzle about American theatre audiences. We know from survey data conducted by the Broadway League, the trade association for theatre owners and producers, that the average age of the non-musical audience member in 2011–2012 was 53 (the musical theatre crowd was on average 43).[19] As Catherine Peterson, the executive director of ArtsBoston, notes, "We know that baby boomers are overrepresented" in theatre audiences, and that "The under-30s are underrepresented."[20] Likewise, the Broadway League's demographic study of the 2011–2012 season reveals that the audience was 78% white.[21] So reception is, and will be, skewed by the non-diverse audiences, who, as Don Aucoin writes, "aren't getting any younger."[22]

It is instructive to read a specific response from an audience member to work through the dynamic nature of reception: reception stems not only from what is presented onstage but also from a complex mix of the individual's personal history, viewing habits, theatrical knowledge, the visual and audible reactions of others in the theatre, and so forth. The example I present comes from the Oregon Shakespeare Festival (OSF), a theatre company that very systematically surveys its audiences regularly, but it should be noted that many small and/or regional theatre companies do not have the resources to conduct audience surveys. As Teresa Eyring, the executive director of the Theatre Communications Group, notes, "For us to get demographic data, our theaters would have to be surveying their audiences on a regular basis, and to do it correctly is quite pricey."[23] While OSF's audience surveys are organized by the marketing department to gain greater knowledge about their audience's demographics in the form of quantitative data (ages, incomes, zip codes, races, numbers of visits to OSF, amounts spent per visit, etc.), the surveys also invite qualitative responses in sections that allow for "additional comments."

One patron's response in this open-ended section of the survey provides not only a useful example of the reception of the typical theatre patron (a 66-year-old, white male), but also the double-bind for political Shakespeares. Not writing about a specific performance in particular but about his overall response to OSF's approach, he lamented,

> I am greatly saddened by what I perceive as the steadily declining quality of the Shakespeare productions. I understand the desire of a director to incorporate his originality into a production. If I have seen *King Lear* five times, I am not distressed to see a sixth production

with varied outlook. However, to the many members of the audience who will see this *Lear* (for example) once in their lives, this is unfair. No director should feel apologetic about producing a traditional presentation if it is done well.[24]

Although this patron is an experienced theatregoer who has seen many and varied productions of Shakespeare, his expectations still govern how he defines the parameters of a "traditional presentation." Moreover, these expectations define what he believes are the acceptable parameters for an audience member's *first* encounter with Shakespeare: "a traditional presentation ... well done."

If I may push your point about reception a bit further, the OSF production to which this patron is responding may have been directed by someone with a very specific political angle (e.g. a modernized setting for *Lear* that comments on our society's approach to dementia and ageing). Nonetheless, this patron resists the political framework because he expects something else. So, how can we more accurately understand expectations? If, as this example demonstrates, expectations determine the parameters of acceptability and authenticity for any given audience member, how exactly are these horizons of expectation formed? Is it a first encounter narrative? If so, does that mean our efforts should focus on introducing political theatre to the very young so their horizons of expectation are politicized? Moreover, how exactly (and practically) do theatrical expectations change over time? Does it happen equally through radical shifts as through gradual changes? And how do we know? While I have employed the survey response above as a way to gauge and engage with reception, I think it is fair to ask how best (financially, ethically, socially) to assess reception. How exactly do we assess the political impact on any given audience? These questions, I think, are central to understanding how theatre companies can and should approach their visions not only of political theatre but also their representations of race, gender, and sexuality on stage.

Of course, I must ask the chicken and egg question as well. Which came first, the traditional Shakespeare production or the audience member who expects a traditional Shakespeare production? While this may seem to be a simplistic question with an easy answer—production must by necessity come first—we know that reception and production are deeply entwined. Reception creates production just as often as production creates reception. Theatre companies across the country are concerned that their patrons are not diversifying. In fact, there is reason to believe that audiences will continue to segregate, age, and dwindle. As Don Aucoin writes, "The need to reach young audiences has long been the subject of much private fretting by artistic directors and other theater professionals. It's a challenge that, if met, might help address the lack of diversity that also afflicts many theaters."[25] While I know that producing the best theatre artistically must be at the top of every theatre company's list of objectives and goals, I wonder if twenty-first century theatre companies are actually creating expectations or simply catering to existing ones, especially with regards to Shakespeare. If theatre companies are concerned with not alienating their existing audience pools, how can they also effectively appeal to younger and more diverse audiences?

Thinking through these questions, I wonder how much marketing fits into your understanding of political theatre. It seems that the marketing department in any given theatre company will play a crucial role in blurring, obscuring, and/or defining the lines between the familiar and the alien on stage. While many non-professional and/or school productions will not employ a marketing team, marketing is performed by every company that wants an audience for its show. Whether it is glossy press releases, professionally developed websites, Facebook posts, Twitter accounts, printed flyers, Kickstarter, or any number of actions undertaken to promote a show, someone intentionally frames the show for those they want to attend. How do we as scholars engage with the marketing efforts employed by theatre companies to understand and analyse if/how political theatre is framed? If it is framed intentionally, then how can we more accurately understand how this framing—whether professional or ad hoc—impacts reception? Likewise, how can we more accurately understand how reception—whether professional or overheard—impacts marketing?

Act 3: Empowerment is all

At this point, I am left asking a rather large question about what the ultimate goal of a political Shakespeare production should be. You deftly address the hydra's head of goals for subversive theatre by stating that relevance should be thrown over for ownership. You write that the goal should be

> ownership, a sense that Shakespeare (or anything else with hegemonic associations) might actually be theirs after all and might be made to speak their ideas, their concerns, their values.... As such, political theatre cannot be defined solely as offering commentary on

or critique of current socio/-economic conditions or military actions, and must also be allowed to serve as a form of empowerment in itself.

Once again I find myself in complete agreement with you. Empowerment must be the goal of political theatre; it must enable agency on political, social, and personal levels. And yet, I am not certain how to square all the competing statements that "X is all."

Let me once again turn to a few specific examples to demonstrate my query. Amy Scott-Douglas writes very movingly about the Shakespeare Behind Bars prison programme in the Luther Luckett Correctional Complex in LaGrange, Kentucky. Explaining the casting practice employed, Scott-Douglas writes,

> What matters more than anything else, they will tell you, is who is the best actor for the part. This, of course, is the mantra of colorblind casting in commercial theatre, but the unspoken and subjective criteria for what makes an actor the "best" actor in commercial theatre is hard to measure. In prison theatre, the criteria are very clear. The best actor for the part is the one whose history is the most similar to the character he or she is playing.[26]

Thus, the focus in this prison programme is on the individual's exploration through a Shakespearean character whose narrative most resembles his/her own. The Shakespeare Behind Bars mission statement, after all, is "to offer theatrical encounters with personal and social issues to the incarcerated, allowing them to develop life skills that will ensure their successful reintegration into society."[27] As you argue, Shakespeare prison programmes are often empowering (as demonstrated in the participants' lower than average recidivism rates).

But I must ask, whither reception in this scenario? Needless to say, Shakespeare prison productions are seen by relatively few audience members. How can reception be all if the attention in Shakespeare prison programmes (with their astonishingly long rehearsal periods) is almost entirely on the individual? "Shakespeare Behind Bars uses the healing power of the arts, transforming inmate offenders from who they were when they committed their crimes, to who they are in the present moment, to who they wish to become."[28] In other words, the work done in these Shakespeare prison programmes is for the individual inmate, not necessarily for the few who may ultimately see the final product.

This example puts me in mind of lots of actors of colour who have attempted to harness Shakespeare's cultural capital to empower themselves. The lineage of black, male Shakespeare actors, for instance, is fascinating both in terms of the stories of individual advancements (financially and socially) and in terms of the lack of larger social advancements. One could safely argue that the trajectory of these individual actors does not necessarily map onto larger social advances. In the nineteenth century, Ira Aldridge, the first black, American actor to gain international success as a classical actor, was hosted by royalty and politicians throughout Eastern Europe; he gained international fame and died in 1867 in Poland, where his grave is tended by the Society of Polish Artists of Film and Theatre. Shakespeare clearly opened doors for Aldridge, but can we map his personal empowerment to a larger social empowerment?

Therefore, I must ask if there are different types of political theatre: ones that empower the actors or company members (e.g. prison programmes), ones that empower the audience (e.g. touring productions in schools), and ones that empower social groups (e.g. the Harlem Shakespeare Festival)? While you write about these different types of political theatre in incredibly effective ways, I wonder how comfortably they all fit under the same rubric of political. After all, there appear to be different goals when the lens shifts focus from individuals to audience members to society writ large. So I must ask empowerment for whom and to what effect? If there are different subsets of political theatre, how do we abide by the maxims you spell out: context is all, reception is all, and empowerment is all?

Your self-conscious shift from a focus on "relevance" to "empowerment" puts me in mind of a different self-conscious shift that you cite early in the book: Baz Kershaw's rejoinder to shift from political theatre to radical theatre. In working through the divides between modernism and post-modernism, Kershaw advises that " 'radical performance' might usefully replace 'political theatre', not because it will enable us to somehow settle the issues raised by the promiscuity of the political in post-modernism, but rather because it will allow us to more directly encounter them."[29] He continues, "the radical can encompass both the fundamental change and the uncertainty of outcome signaled by the post-modern and post-modernity."[30] Radical performance, then, invokes not simply "freedom from oppression, repression, exploitation—the resistant sense of the radical—but also freedom to reach beyond existing systems of formalized power, freedom to create currently unimaginable forms of association and action—the transgressive or transcendent sense of the radical."[31]

While you cite Kershaw's arguments and terminology, ultimately you do not employ them within the book. I wonder how you see your political Shakespeares as diverging from Kershaw's radical performance. I find that Kershaw's argument provides a way to incorporate the Eden Troupe at Patrick Henry College into our discussion of political Shakespeares because radical performances have "no necessary ideological tendency" and can be embraced by "both Left and Right factions in contemporary politics."[32] Likewise, he eschews discussions of empowerment for discussions of "vigorous and fundamental change."[33] I point you in this direction not because I think Kershaw has answered all the questions I have posed to you; his focus is not particularly helpful when one is working through contemporary performances of Shakespeare in a multicultural world. Instead, I point us towards his terms because I think they might help to broaden our scope of the political. Neither context, reception nor empowerment can be all; rather, the inspiration of vigorous dialogue in the hope of fundamental change(s) may be all.

Andrew James Hartley

A preliminary response

Many thanks for this provocative and observant response, Ayanna. Let me address each of your "acts" in turn.

Context is all

You are right, of course, to point out that not all political theatre is leftist theatre. Early in the writing of the book I considered tackling right-leaning theatre, but opted not to, partly because I assumed my academic readership would be aware of the way mainstream theatre tilts towards the conservative and partly because I find that kind of material just too exasperating, but your point is a good one, and your example intriguing. It strikes me as telling that the school in question was not established until this century. Before then, it seems to me, conservative religious schools tended to frame their agenda in spiritual, cultural, and moral terms, and while what they were advocating was in fact political, it took the visibility of the Tea Party movement and vocal right-wing Christian elements in the post-9/11 years to reshape the debate in expressly and self-consciously political terms. As editor of *Shakespeare Bulletin*, I had a run-in with a conservative Christian university which sought to block publication of one of our reviews of its campus Shakespeare productions because school administrators took issue with our reviewer's political reading of both their work and their active support of George W. Bush's administration. Their claim was—bizarrely, to my mind—that neither their productions nor the school's overall stance were in any way political, since they framed their college's overall culture in terms of "values" rather politics. Perhaps we should be glad that Patrick Henry College are at least up front about their political agenda.

As someone who was raised as a northern English Catholic in a working class area, I continue to find the right-leaning assumptions behind much US Christianity baffling. Where I grew up, religion (some of it in the liberation theology mode) was expressly leftist in its agenda, its driving political force geared to issues of social justice at home and abroad, this—in part, at least—because it was assumed that how one treated others was more important (even for salvation) than what one believed. Which is to say that I don't assume religiously driven Shakespeare to be inherently conservative any more than I would consider Shakespeare itself to be so. So again, I suppose, context really is all. That we need to be mindful of overtly conservative production agendas, I freely concede, even if much of what they have to offer feels old hat or simple-minded; the amount of *Macbeth* which gets fudged when we turn it into a morally binary depiction of back-sliding into paganism boggles the mind, as well as making the play into historical nonsense. No doubt similar objections could be raised to some leftist productions, but the company agenda at places like Patrick Henry seems to me more barefaced, more reductive, more obvious than left-leaning companies whose approach is to challenge, to own, to subvert. I understand that some conservatives don't think there is a difference between going into rehearsals with such a mission, but I disagree, thinking that the leftist position tends to be more interrogatory and dialectical than is the religiously conservative company whose mandate is the promotion of biblical truths.[34]

As to the Brustein/Wilson debate, and the link between discussions centring on the conceptual directing of Shakespeare to larger issues in theatre, I would begin by saying that I suspect all absolute dictums about what makes for good and bad theatre are usually wrong. Brustein's binary sense of conceptual directing seems to me simplistic. It is all too easy to imagine productions which move between simile and metaphor, even on a moment-to-moment basis, and I would assert again W.B. Worthen's observation that all production is (necessarily, generically) adaptation, the degrees of which must be assessed in the particulars of the show as received and understood by the (plural) audience. I respect Wilson's position on cross-racial casting and accept that the argument had to be made, but (again) its absolute nature bothers me. I avoid racial cross-casting in my own theatrical work when it might imply the irrelevance of race, but I'm sceptical of the idea that it always necessarily undermines the historical identity of the black actor. Where Shakespeare is concerned, such a position seems to imply that while black actors come from a separate tradition, another social group is the natural heir to Shakespeare. I don't know who that latter group is anymore, and I think our political will is best spent breaking such assumptions down. As a director and dramaturg I'm a pragmatist: if a particular play or character cannot be made usefully provocative or palatable, then I probably wouldn't want to be involved in the show. I feel the same way about cross-racial or -gendered casting. I'll evaluate it on a case-by-case basis, and while I realize (as both a theatre practitioner and a critic) that such individual cases cannot overturn the political legacy which surrounds them, I am prepared to consider the possibility that the nuance of such details might productively complicate the moment and the assumptions attendant on it.

Reception is all

You put your finger on some serious problems here, and I can only offer the beginnings of answers. Your instance of the audience complaint reminds me of a woman who once remarked to me that she hoped to see every Shakespeare play on stage once before she died. As we talked it became clear that she hadn't really considered that every production was different and that it made (from my perspective) as much sense to shoot to see as many different *Hamlet*s as possible as it did to see single productions of different plays. There is, of course, no such thing as a definitive production, and while not fully processing this might be understandable for people who don't see much theatre, one would expect a seasoned theatregoer to have a more sophisticated understanding. I suspect that your quoted critic actually does, though he or she chooses to ignore it in pursuit of a more "traditional" production which would more clearly replicate his or her politics or—more likely—allow the audience to conceive of the show as somehow apolitical in the manner of that conservative Christian school I referenced above. I don't agree that a "traditional" or "straight" (ha!) *Lear* is better for an audience because I don't believe that the function of the production is to teach the play. The production is its own work of art and should not be obligated to enact all perspectives on the play, doubly so when "traditional" is code for a political perspective the director or company finds repellant. It seems to me telling that in this case the complaint begins by bewailing the "quality" of the production, suggesting that the issue might be about the execution of the director's ideas by actors or designers, perhaps, but ends confessing that the issue was that the production was not "traditional." This is one of those irregular verbs, isn't it? My taste in Shakespeare values quality. Yours is jollied up. His is a travesty. We should, as you know, never mistake such statements of taste—especially political taste—for anything grander, more objective, or connected to issues of inherent worth.

That ignoring politically retrograde critique risks alienating the audience, I accept. Indeed, I embrace it. And yes, I am able to because I am not trying to keep a theatre company afloat and therefore terrified of losing audience members (one of the pleasures of working mainly for a university company whose audience is largely students and their families). But I mean it when I ask at what point does placating the retrograde sympathies of your audience undermine the very purpose of your existence? If a company is not free artistically and politically, then why bother staying afloat at all? Proselytizing Shakespeare is not a good enough reason to justify a company's continued existence, particularly if the form your Shakespeare takes actually reaffirms principles you believe invalid or damaging. Can your sense of audience modulate your approach, so that you can take the majority of them with you, even when the production pushes their political envelope? Absolutely. I am not advocating a frontal assault on your community's values. Here, as elsewhere, I value nuance, teasing, provocation, and careful, sensitive navigation as much as I do bold statement, particularly where the former is the spoonful of sugar and the latter merely a barrel of vinegar. But yes: if you have to throw out your principles to make art, what's the point?

Your observations on audience demographics are well taken, however, and I'm very aware of the constant struggle to draw in younger audiences. What I also see in the United States, however, is regional companies trying to draw in younger audiences with slick and sexy marketing, only to then offer them the same staid and pedestrian fare on stage which they have been pedalling for decades. Partly this is a fear of moving on from what has kept them solvent in the past and what their elderly audience seem to like, but it indicates both a disconnect from and a lack of respect for the younger audience they supposedly want to attract, an audience which can be lured with high gloss tricks but whose actual world is not being considered or represented in the production itself. To companies who really want to draw a younger crowd I would say: hire new directors, rethink the brand of Shakespeare you intend to put on stage, and build your marketing around that. In such re-evaluation, politics in its broadest sense should be integral as should, perhaps, a sense of what theatre itself might be. We have grown so used to bemoaning the dwindling of theatre audiences that we don't spend enough time wondering if it is not the absentee audience's fault but ours in failing to recognize the way arts and entertainment culture has changed, particularly with the technological innovations of the last two decades. The music industry, film, TV, journalism, and book publishing have all been wrestling with these changes for some time and the shifting landscape has altered not just how people process their art and entertainment, but what that art and entertainment is. These are challenging times demanding creative solutions, but to use the various pressures on theatre companies to justify the gutting of politics in our stage Shakespeare seems to me utterly wrong-headed.

Empowerment is all

Well yes, as you point out, I'm having my cake and eating it too in claiming that various things are "all" important. I can't have it all ways at once, and the reception/empowerment contradiction makes that clear, as does the Ira Aldridge example which shows how individual empowerment may not have larger social reach. I think you have already anticipated my answer to this dilemma, of course, which falls back on that sense of the plurality, diversity, and specificity of individual productions. The goals of each show, its marks of success, vary from production to production. In a prison or a classroom or an experimental lab show, the empowerment of those involved may trump whatever an audience (if there even is one) gets out of the experience. By contrast, I think the individual experience of the cast in most professional productions is largely irrelevant to my assessment of their achievement. I know that I can't have it all for any single production, but I do insist upon a range of assessment criteria whose importance fluctuates significantly from staging to staging, maybe even from scene to scene or moment to moment.

I would extend this argument to readings of a given production. Recently a colleague came to me to quibble about the way love was represented in a production of *Romeo and Juliet* for which I was dramaturg. "Where was the darkness, the failure, the miscommunication which makes you realize it was all futile?" he asked.

"But this show wasn't interested in those things," I said. This production believed in the love between the protagonists and set them against the darkness of an oppressively cynical, adult culture resolving around the abuse of power through technology (and it was very well received by those coveted younger audiences). I thought my colleague's reading of the play perfectly valid as a reading and as a way of teaching the play, but it was not the play we had decided to stage, and that seems to me perfectly acceptable. To try to make a production do everything that the play text might be seen to do is a theoretical and practical impossibility. But—to come back to where we begun—that is only a problem if you assume that the production must somehow be the play in a definitive sense, rather than a new theatrical event which is both a manifestation of the play and a response to it.

So, yes. There are different kinds of political theatre, as many, perhaps, as there are productions, and their goals and achievements vary. Your chicken/egg question about which comes first, the traditional production or the audience who expects/craves it, leads me to a perverse answer. What comes first is the text, not in the sense that the text somehow contains the parameters of the performance, but in the sense that most audience members come to Shakespeare through the schoolroom first, and the theatre second. The extent to which this shapes expectations, senses of rightness and authenticity, but also of empowerment and other forms of politics, cannot be overestimated. And I agree that the political outcome—or radical outcome (in Kershaw's sense)—we can best look for as these cultural assumptions meet the material practice of Shakespeare on stage, is the development of rigorous dialogue which re-examines, counters, undermines what we thought we knew as we move into what I hope will be a more tolerant, equal, and progressive culture. For me there is no paradox in the notion that the nano-details of individual performances of Shakespeare might be components in the social and political changes to come.

Ayanna Thompson

Concluding thoughts

Andrew, I think it is incredibly useful to emphasize that no one production should be seen/treated as definitive, and the example you provide about the 37-play cycle goal versus the 37 *Hamlets* goal is a perfectly instructive one. Many people (including myself) want to see all 37 plays in performance, but that goal implicitly locates authority and authenticity in the individual production (i.e. each production becomes THE play). While I am not one who typically falls in the trap of authenticity (I am usually labelled as an iconoclast), the lure of the aggregate Shakespeare (seeing all the plays in performance) is a strong one that should be interrogated. Where did I get this idea? When did this become a goal? How was this desire informed, shaped, and/or created?

These questions, of course, lead us back to taste, expectations, and reception. For scholars and practitioners, the dwindling, ageing, and segregating audiences for live theatre must be a concern. We must find better ways to partner with educators at the primary, secondary, and collegiate levels to make political Shakespeares the new tradition. I deliberately lump these educators together because all too often college and university professors do not see their teaching of Shakespeare as operating in the same vein as primary and secondary educators. While there are important distinctions to be made (e.g. in speed, depth, and levels of comprehension), there are also important cohesions that ought to be emphasized more systematically. Many educators, for instance, employ performance-based techniques (e.g. the Folger's Shakespeare Set Free approach for primary and secondary educators is performance based), and these approaches are exactly where traditions can be formed or subverted. While many performance-based approaches bill themselves as creating a life-long love of Shakespeare, this is a very conservative goal: love does not equal empowerment. Instead, performance-based programmes should foster a life-long love of interrogation, alteration, and adaptation. If the ultimate goal of political Shakespeares is to empower viewers, practitioners, and/or social groups, then we need to reshape tastes and expectations in the classroom by demonstrating that no one performance or production will provide the truth, the answer, or Shakespeare's intention. Political Shakespeares will only succeed if we retrain our palates to enjoy his "infinite varieties."

Andrew James Hartley

Concluding thoughts

Yes, Ayanna, I agree with your sense of educators sharing common goals and that these should be geared towards empowerment, and I'd like to extend your point about recognizing that a "love of Shakespeare" is a political goal. One of the problems with literary and theatrical culture in the popular mindset is that analysis of politics is too often minimized, disguised (as we have already said) as a discussion of moral or social "values," or dodged entirely in favour of aesthetic or emotional concerns, often foregrounding individual relationships as if they existed in a political vacuum. If we can advocate—on stage and in the classroom—for the recognition, the embrace of Shakespeare as a fundamentally political entity, not the apolitically "timeless" or "universal" genius of Western literary tradition, and marry that recognition with the aforementioned sense that every production is a new production, an adaptation which can never be definitive, then maybe we will be able to see Shakespeare as theoretically and practically malleable in expressly—and usefully—political terms. Perhaps then we will discover a paradoxical newness and immediacy, stemming not from those old assumptions of universality but from the direct and formative interaction of our own cultural moment, audiences, students, and theatre practitioners with the richness of the plays. Perhaps also that interaction will—in generating an energized, politicized Shakespeare—render moot all those anxieties about dwindling audiences and failing relevance.

Part IV
Annotated Reading List

For ease of reference, I have divided the following list into three sections—on reading Shakespeare politically, on political theatre, and on staging Shakespeare—though it is assumed that the student of the larger subject will find overlap and cross-pollination between all three areas. The list is far from exhaustive but should provide provocative starting points for readers who want to explore further the ideas surrounding Shakespeare and political theatre.

Reading Shakespeare politically

Jonathan Dollimore and Alan Sinfield, eds., *Political Shakespeare: New Essays in Cultural Materialism*. 1985. Manchester: Manchester University Press, 1994. Print.
    A vital collection of essays which applied the material theoretical concerns of gender, race, class, and ideology to the study of Shakespeare, including articles by writers such as Stephen Greenblatt ("Invisible Bullets") which came close to defining the new politicized sense of what Shakespeare was. Notable essays include Paul Brown on The Tempest and the Discourse of Colonialism, Kate McKluskie on Shakespeare and Patriarchy, and the Afterword by Marxist critic Raymond Williams.

Jonathan Dollimore. *Radical Tragedy: Religion, Ideology, and Power in the Drama of Shakespeare and His Contemporaries*. 1984. Durham, NC: Duke University Press, 2004. Print.
    One of the most important books in Shakespeare criticism and one which deals not only with Shakespeare but also with contemporary writers such as Middleton, Marston, Marlowe, and Jonson, painting a picture of early modern theatre as an entity which depicted and undermined

the social structures and ideological pressures of a highly ordered and oppressive society. Dollimore's powerful and readable study of how the plays of the period exposed and unraveled the hierarchical fictions of the Elizabethan and Jacobean periods was one of the flagships of a new wave of political readings of early modern drama whose legacy persists into the present.

John Drakakis, ed. *Alternative Shakespeare*. 1985. New York: Routledge, 2002. Print.
A landmark collection growing out of the theoretical revolutions of the 1970s and 1980s which sought to rethink the nature and purpose of Shakespeare in culture. The book contains essays by such critics as Francis Barker, Catherine Belsey, Jonathan Dollimore, John Drakakis, Keir Elam, Malcolm Evans, Terence Hawkes, Peter Hulme, James Kavanagh, Christopher Norris, Jacqueline Rose, Alessandro Serpieri, and Alan Sinfield.

Political theatre

Benjamin Bennett. *All Theatre Is Revolutionary Theatre*. Ithaca, NY: Cornell University Press, 2005. Print.
A historically arranged philosophical argument aimed at proving—first through abstract analysis of early criticism, then through specific case instances—that "drama, by virtue of its indissoluble association with the brute materiality of theatre, disrupts fundamentally, and opens to the possibility of revolution, the otherwise at least potentially closed system of Western literature" (8). Moving from Aristotle to Robert Wilson via Brecht, Artaud, T.S. Eliot, Georg Buchner, Diderot, George Bernard Shaw, and Samuel Beckett, and ending with a consideration of theatrical hermeneutics, Bennett sets out to show how the problematic qualities of drama shed light on "the question of history and the destiny of totalitarianism" (9). So good luck with that.

Augusto Boal. *Theatre of the Oppressed*. 1979. New York: Theatre Communications Group, 1993. Print.
Starting with a study of Aristotle as the root of an oppressive theatrical model because it renders the audience passive, Boal's most influential book presents his theories and methodologies geared towards a form of theatre which empowers and liberates. He lays out the nature and logic of specific practices such as what he calls newspaper theatre, invisible theatre, analytical theatre, and forum theatre, using specific instances of

actual theatrical practice to ground his ideas. The model of theatre for which he advocates is one geared to the generation of social change by creating a dynamically engaged and constructive audience.

Augusto Boal. *Legislative Theatre*. New York: Routledge, 1998. Print.

An extended consideration of what Boal calls "Forum Theatre" in which the disempowered and voiceless are given a say in community affairs, the making of law, and formulation of local government policy through theatrical exercises, interactive dramaturgy, and the subsequent consideration of the ideas and conflicts which emerge. The book is in part a personal history and is dotted with anecdotes and incidents from Boal's own experience as a theatre maker and legislator in Brazil.

Laura Bradley. *Brecht and Political Theatre: The Mother on Stage*. Oxford: Oxford University Press, 2006. Print.

More than a case study, Bradley's detailed consideration of Brecht's play ranges from its conception and formation as a text, its early stage history, and critical reception to a detailed consideration of its afterlife in theatre theory, criticism, and on various stages all over Europe and the United States through the twentieth century and into the new millennium. Particular emphasis is given to the play's political dimension both in terms of Brecht's own purposes and the way the various productions scrutinized were received.

Baz Kershaw. *The Radical in Performance: Between Brecht and Baudrillard*. New York: Routledge, 1999. Print.

A study of postmodern performance practice's subversive edge and its movement away from more conventional forms of theatre whose political capacity to subvert has become increasingly enfeebled by its irrelevance to contemporary culture. To put it in his words, "[f]ar from showing us the shape of new freedoms, the theatre estate in Britain and elsewhere has transformed itself into a disciplinary marketplace devoted to the systematic evacuation or diffusion of disruptive agencies, oppositional voices and radical programmes for progressive social change" (32). In opposition to such a culture, Kershaw posits a postmodern theatre geared to reinforcing the processes of democracy and, in the book's second part, offers specific sites and means by which his notion of radical performance might be enacted.

Ric Knowles. *Reading the Material Theatre*. Cambridge: Cambridge University Press, 2004. Print.

Knowles's method insists upon considering the entirety of the theatrical experience—from all aspects of its production to the specifics of its reception—in assessing its political semantics. The five case studies on which he focuses pay special attention to issues of funding, casting, venue, and local particularities (especially in the case of touring productions) as generators and destabilizers of cultural meaning and value.

Joe Kelleher. *Theatre and Politics*. New York: Palgrave Macmillan, 2009. Print.

A short, pithy, and readable introduction to the core ideas and problems inherent in bringing theatre and politics together. Kelleher draws on theory from Plato, Ranciere, and others while using an array of specific instances to press into issues of praxis.

Jeanne Colleran and Jenny S. Spencer, eds. *Staging Resistance: Essays on Political Theater*. Ann Arbor, MI: University of Michigan Press, 1998. Print.

A book of essays premised on the need for new paradigms to understand the functionality of political theatre and grounded in a diverse range of individual case studies enacting various forms of cultural struggle. The collection is particularly strong on issues of gender and nationalism.

Richard Boon and Jane Plastow, eds. *Theatre and Empowerment*. Cambridge: Cambridge University Press, 2004. Print.

A collection of essays on specific instances of performance programmes and events from such diverse places as Ethiopia, India, Northern Ireland, South Africa, and Italy. In each case, the performance is contextualized within the social situations of those involved, with the express purpose of exploring and transforming those situations. Though not always successful, each instance—recounted and analysed by a different author—attests to the value of performance as a catalyst for social change.

Zygmunt Hubner. *Theatre & Politics*. Evanston, IL: Northwestern University Press, 1992. Print.

Drawing on his experience in Poland, Hubner presents a critical overview of the history of Western theatre (including the ancient Greeks, the medieval, Elizabethan, and later French and Russian models) and the manner in which it lends itself to political propaganda and subversion. He considers the ways in which audiences can be alert to the sometimes finely nuanced or dangerous political valences of theatre and discusses the specifics of theatre which operates under totalitarian regimes, censorship, and forms of audience resistance.

Peter Thomson and Glendyr Sacks, eds. The *Cambridge Companion to Brecht*. Cambridge: Cambridge University Press, 1994. Print.
   Part biography, part literary analysis of the plays, and part study of his theoretical and practical work, this collection of essays by a wide range of experts is an excellent starting point for anyone looking to learn more about Brecht and his work.

John J. White. *Bertolt Brecht's Dramatic Theory*. Rochester, NY: Camden House, 2004. Print.
   A close examination of Brecht's theoretical writings about theatre in terms of the cultural and ideological context in which he was working, also taking into account subsequent dramatic and aesthetic theory. The whole is shot through with a detailed analysis of his argumentative methods and a consideration of how his ideas shifted and refined as he encountered problems over the course of his career.

Bertolt Brecht. *Brecht on Theatre: The Development of an Aesthetic*. Trans. John Willett. New York: Hill and Wang, 1964. Print.
   A collection of Brecht's writings on theatre spanning the period from 1918 to 1956. This is a useful resource for the student who wants to see how Brecht developed and refined his various ideas and theories about theatre practice, particularly his evolving notion of key ideas such as Epic theatre and the alienation effect.

Shakespeare on stage

James. C. Bulman, ed. *Shakespeare Re-Dressed: Cross-Gender Casting in Contemporary Performance*. Madison, NJ: Fairleigh Dickinson University Press, 2008. Print.
   An essay collection exploring the many different forms of cross-gendered casting in Shakespeare performance in ways elucidating matters of gender politics, sexual orientation, and other forms of "transgressive" behaviour facilitated and scrutinized by the plays in contemporary production.

Amy Scott Douglas. *Shakespeare Inside: The Bard Behind Bars*. London: Continuum Press, 2007. Print.

A short, intensely personal book of essays on prison Shakespeare. Some chapters are close-up looks at individual actors/inmates while others focus on individual events/productions, issues/ideas, and interviews with practitioners and other key players, including a warden. The tone is often healthily sceptical, but genuinely engaged and unafraid of revealing the author's intellectual and emotional presence in the lives and events she scrutinizes.

Andrew James Hartley. *The Shakespearean Dramaturg: A Theoretical and Practical Guide for the Scholar in the Theatre.* Basingstoke: Palgrave Macmillan, 2005. Print.

An attempt to marry recent critical thought with actual theatrical practice from the perspective of the production dramaturg. The first part represents relevant theoretical issues as they apply to the staging of Shakespeare, while the second explores specific issues such as script editing, working with actors on textual issues, generating usable research, programme notes and other matters in which the dramaturg might help guide the production's intellectual dimension.

Barbara Hodgdon and W.B. Worthen, eds. *A Companion to Shakespeare and Performance.* Hoboken, NJ: Wiley-Blackwell, 2008. Print.

An impressive collection with essays from 34 leading voices in the field covering a wide range of subjects from performance terminology, history, the material conditions of staging, pedagogy, and the theatrical dimension of identity and its political associations.

James Loehlin. *Henry V: Shakespeare in Performance.* Manchester: Manchester University Press, 2000. Print.

Lois Potter. *Othello: Shakespeare in Performance.* Manchester: Manchester University Press, 2002.

These and other books in the same series focus on individual plays and their recent history on stage and screen, identifying trends in performance, and the ways that productions have engaged with the evolving—often political—discourse surrounding the play. Each book provides a set of examples of how different productions have interpreted and constructed the play in their own individual manner, focusing largely on twentieth- and twenty-first century productions in ways foregrounding contemporary issues and ideas.

W.B. Worthen. *Shakespeare and the Authority of Performance.* Cambridge: Cambridge University Press, 1997. Print.

A ground-breaking book which almost single-handedly revolutionized the thinking about what Shakespeare on stage is by bringing a range of theoretical innovations to a subject area which had been remarkably unselfconscious in terms of critical rigour. Worthen grapples particularly with the strategies used to legitimize Shakespeare on stage, interrogating the relationship between authorship and authority in the way theatre makes meaning out of the plays.

Dennis Kennedy. *Looking at Shakespeare: A Visual History of Twentieth-Century Performance.* 2nd ed. Cambridge: Cambridge University Press, 2001. Print.
A nicely illustrated overview of Shakespeare on stage in Europe, Japan, and North America, rendered in terms of design and rooted in the aesthetic movements of the modern and postmodern, which offers a deft corrective to the notion that Shakespeare is defined verbally and textually.

Carol Rutter. *Clamorous Voices: Shakespeare's Women Today.* London: Women's Pr Ltd., 1994. Print.
A collection of lively and provocative interviews and discussion with five prominent actresses (Harriet Walter, Juliet Stevenson, Paola Dionisetti, Fiona Shaw, and Sinead Cusack) on playing Shakespeare's most dynamic and interesting female roles. Rather than simply being ruminations on scripted characters, these discussions foreground choices, attitudes, and the material conditions of various productions in their sense of what those characters are or might be.

Ayannna Thompson and Ania Loomba, eds. *Colorblind Shakespeare: New Perspectives on Race and Performance,* New York: Routledge, 2006. Print.
A collection of 14 essays on the history, theory, practice, and political controversy surrounding "colour-blind" casting, in ways navigating the nature of the plays' original performance conditions and subsequent cultural developments. The book focuses on changing notions of race and its representation on stage and explores the desirability and practicality of non-traditional racial casting in political terms.

Sarah Werner. *New Directions in Renaissance Drama and Performance Studies,* New York: Palgrave Macmillan, 2010. Print.
An essay collection by important scholars of Shakespeare in performance on with a range of subjects from dealing with the ephemeral, reconnecting literary criticism and performance analysis, and the

contemporary resituating of performed Shakespeare in the larger cultural and scholarly world.

Jean Trounstine. *Shakespeare Behind Bars: The Power of Drama in a Women's Prison*. New York: St. Martin's Press, 2001. Print.

A documentary and often novelistic account of the author's work with inmates at Framingham Women's Prison in Massachusetts during their work on an adaptation of *The Merchant of Venice*.

Notes

1. The Politics of the Stage

1. This is particularly the case with his 1930 *Mahagonny* notes which have tended to render static and unhistorical statements of Brecht's theoretical beliefs which he revisited and modified later in life. This is addressed expressly in John White's *Bertolt Brecht's Dramatic Theory* 28–31. See also Laura Bradley.
2. As Augusto Boal points out, Brecht's use of the term "epic" is itself Hegelian and problematic, based as it is on an idealist poetics in which the spirit of the individual shapes social reality, rather than the other way round. Boal prefers the term Marxist Poetics to define Brecht's position (*Theatre of the Oppressed* 92–94).
3. Hubner was also critical of Brecht for his support of state-sponsored communism, and when Brecht's stylistic methodology fell foul of Soviet criticism—wedded as the state and its mouthpieces were to the crudest and most idealizing forms of socialist realism—Hubner says Brecht "deserved all the scolding he received" (141).
4. I will return to this idea in my consideration of *Henry V* in Chapter 3 (Part II).

2. The Curious Case of Mr Shakespeare

1. See Jill Dolan.
2. See Edward W. Said.
3. Such ideas are also the starting point for African American theatre scholars such as Harry J. Elam, Jr and David Krasner whose *African American Performance and Theater History: A Critical Reader* provides an excellent sampling of critical writing from the field.
4. For a sense of New Historicism, see the work of Stephen Greenblatt, Leonard Tennenhouse, and Stephen Orgel.
5. For examples of Cultural Materialism, see the work of Jonathan Dollimore, Alan Sinfield, and Graham Holderness.
6. See Keith Booker.
7. Garber is responding here to critiques of the academy's political inflection and to the remark by African American poet Maya Angelou, utilized as an attack on that inflection, that Shakespeare spoke for her as a black woman, that to all intents and purposes he *was* a black woman, this in spite of Shakespeare's manifestation of racist and misogynist discourse (Garber 74).
8. See Michael Taylor's "The Critical Tradition."
9. For an extended consideration of this issue, see Ayanna Thompson's *Colorblind Shakespeare: New Perspectives on Race and Performance.*
10. I shall return to this issue in Chapter 3.

11. See Lizbeth Goodman.
12. See for instance "On Queering Twelfth Night."

3. Identity Politics and the Stage

1. For her part, Werner found the production usefully feminist in its approach, though only in retrospect, seeing in its theatrical strategies an exposing of various gendered structures which hinged on the audience desire for a happy ending. The production refused to "solve" the play, but drew attention to its fantasy of female containment in ways pressing the audience to scrutinize their own expectations and desires. This subtle and complex reading was, Werner is quick to point out, not one the newspaper critics recognized (84–90).
2. Thompson uses a particularly fruitful example in which black comedian Dave Chappelle took the laughter of one white audience member in response to his blackface skit as being somehow "wrong." Instead of parodying stereotypes, Chappelle felt that he was unwittingly confirming them because he could not determine how his audience would read what they were seeing (104).
3. This extract is taken from "My Problem with Shylock," a brief online adjunct piece for the production Mazer was dramaturging. An extended consideration of the process and Mazer's own dramaturgical struggles with the anti-Semitic issues which the production encountered in rehearsals are tellingly laid out in a two-part essay entitled "Solanio's Coin."
4. For a consideration of audience demographics and ticket pricing, see my essays "Shakespeare and Contemporary Performance Spaces."
5. Though I saw the production in person I'm indebted to Elizabeth Klett for refreshing my memory in her "Re-Dressing the Balance: All-Female Shakespeare at the Globe Theatre."

4. "Who talks of my nation?" Challenging the Establishment

1. Others, of course, bemoaned this very factor, wishing instead for something more obviously theatrical and driven by the sound of the language (see Loehlin, *Henry V*).
2. I am indebted here, as elsewhere in this chapter, to James Loehlin's account of the production.
3. See for instance *The Roots of Football Hooliganism: An Historical and Sociological Study*.
4. For a thorough consideration of the production's political valences in its Toronto transfer, see Knowles 166–179.
5. Stuart Hampton Reeves explains the funding structure which, paradoxically, was the kind of mixture of public and private funding the government wanted to see extended across the arts. See *The Henry VI Plays*.
6. See Todd Landon Barnes.
7. See Ben Brantley's New York Times review of February 15th, 2008.
8. See for instance Michael Miller's review for the Berkshire Review.

9. Orson Welles directed the so-called *"Voodoo" Macbeth* at the Federal Theatre Project in New York in 1936. Though the administrative staff were all white, the show used an all black cast and transported the play's Scottish setting to an island modelled on Haiti. Most of the actors had limited experience with Shakespeare, but the production was received enthusiastically, was praised for its energy and innovation, and was one of the successes which put its young director on the map.
10. For details of the production, see Todd Landon Barnes' review for *Shakespeare Bulletin*.

5. "Let him be Caesar": Representing Politics

1. See for instance Robert S. Miola's "Julius Caesar and the Tyrannicide Debate" and Wayne Rebhorn's "The Crisis of the Aristocracy in Julius Caesar."
2. I have already referenced Brecht's extended discussion of the opening crowd scene in *Coriolanus* (see *Brecht on Theatre* 252–265).
3. For more detailed consideration of these and subsequent productions of the play, see my *Julius Caesar* (Shakespeare in Performance series).

6. Place and Pedagogy: Site-Specific Production, School Tours, Prison Shakespeare, and the Question of Agenda

1. See Pierre Bourdieu.
2. See Evelyn B. Tribble and John Sutton on the way that memory and cognition generates multiply located temporal experience.
3. My own personal evidence comes from various institutions in the American southeast, including school outreach by my own institution, the University of North Carolina at Charlotte (whose faculty directed, student acted *Twelfth Night* toured area high schools in 2011), and touring shows performed by the Atlanta-based professional company, Georgia Shakespeare, whose education department provided me with post-production student questionnaires.
4. One instance I have already discussed which concerns how students might "own" Shakespeare is the discussion of the African American Shakespeare Company's *Macbeth* in Chapter 4.
5. Books on this subject include Milla Cozart Riggio's, *Teaching Shakespeare Through Performance*; Ralph Alan Coen's *ShakesFear and How to Cure It!*, and Edward Rocklin's, *Performance Approaches to Teaching Shakespeare*. Other resources can be found through the British Shakespeare Association's education-specific website http://shakespeareineducation.com/.
6. See Jean Trounstine.
7. See Amy Scott Douglas.
8. See Kirk Melnikoff's review of the *Shakespeare Behind Bars* film.
9. Ramona Wray's compelling article on this film takes a radically different tack than mine here, exploring the film as a piece of politically specific art rather than focusing on the transformative power of the process itself on the lives of the prisoners. Wray makes a potent case against the universalizing hagiography inherent in much of the Shakespeare-in-prison discourse. See "The

Morals of *Macbeth* and Peace as Process: Adapting Shakespeare in Northern Ireland's Maximum Security Prison."
10. See the promotional video on the program's main website. http://www.shakespearebehindbars.org/index.htm.
11. That sense that Shakespeare is "safe" and suitable for teaching has made it particularly popular with the latest incarnation of the governmental Shakespeare in American Communities initiative—now renamed Shakespeare for a New Generation. Since 2004 the project has become expressly youth focused, aiming to help "to build future audiences by educating and inspiring students to become informed theatregoers and active participants within the arts and civic organizations that bring distinction to their communities." In keeping with its emphasis on "at-risk" students and those already incarcerated, this new incarnation of the programme is also funded by the Office of Juvenile Justice and Delinquency Prevention, U.S. Department of Justice. http://www.shakespeareinamericancommunities.org/about.

8. "A Conversation with Ayanna Thompson in Three Acts"

1. The Patrick Henry College mission statement can be found on their website: http://www.phc.edu/mission.php.
2. Hanna Rosin, "God and Country," *The New Yorker*, June 27, 2005.
3. Ibid.
4. Quoted in Rosin, "God and Country."
5. http://www.phc.edu/20120315_edentroupe.php.
6. http://www.phc.edu/edentroupe.php.
7. http://www.phc.edu/drama.php.
8. http://www.phc.edu/20090313.php.
9. http://www.phc.edu/edentroupe_macbeth.php.
10. http://www.phc.edu/alumni_wright_a.php.
11. Ibid.
12. http://www.phc.edu/edentroupe_twelfthnight.php.
13. http://www.phc.edu/edentroupe.php.
14. Robert Brustein, "Reworking the Classics: Homage or Ego Trip?" *New York Times*, November 6, 1988.
15. Brustein, "Reworking the Classics."
16. Ibid.
17. August Wilson, *The Ground on Which I Stand* (Theater Communications Group, 1996), 31.
18. Brustein, "Reworking the Classics: Homage or Ego Trip?"
19. "Who Goes to Broadway?" *The Demographics of the Broadway Audience 2011–2012 Season* (The Broadway League, 2012).
20. Quoted in Don Aucoin, "Phantom of the Theater: Audience is Getting Older," *Boston Globe*, June 17, 2012.
21. "Who Goes to Broadway?" *The Demographics of the Broadway Audience 2011–2012 Season*.
22. Aucoin, "Phantom of the Theater: Audience is Getting Older."
23. Quoted in Aucoin, "Phantom of the Theater."

24. 1991 OSF Audience Survey.
25. Aucoin, "Phantom of the Theateren."
26. Amy Scott-Douglass, "Shades of Shakespeare: Colorblind Casting and Interracial Couples in *Macbeth in Manhattan, Grey's Anatomy*, and Prison Macbeth." In *Weyward Macbeth: Intersections of Race and Performance,* edited by Scott L. Newstok and Ayanna Thompson (Palgrave Macmillan, 2010), 200.
27. http://www.shakespearebehindbars.org/about/mission/.
28. Ibid.
29. Baz Kershaw, *The Radical in Performance: Between Brecht and Baudrillard* (Routledge, 1999), 17.
30. Ibid., 17.
31. Ibid., 18.
32. Ibid., 18.
33. Raymond Williams cited by Kershaw, *The Radical in Performance*, 18.
34. A similar binary might be observed in contemporary music. That which self-identifies as Christian rock is—to my mind—almost always less interesting than its secular counterpart because the music is less an end in itself than it is a vehicle for a predetermined orthodox message which cannot be challenged or questioned without the song ceasing to be Christian rock.

Bibliography

"About the Program." *Shakespeare in American Communities.* n.d., n.p. Web.
"About Us." *African American Shakespeare Company.* 2012. Web.
Atkins, Kim, Ed. *Self and Subjectivity.* Blackwell Readings in Continental Philosophy 8. Malden, MA: Blackwell Publishing, 2005. Print.
Barnes, Todd Landon. "George W. Bush's Three Shakespeares: Macbeth, Macbush, and the Theater of War." *Shakespeare Bulletin* 26.3 (2008). Print.
——. "Review." *Shakespeare Bulletin* 27.3 (2009): 461–468. Print.
Bennett, Benjamin. *All Theatre Is Revolutionary Theatre.* Ithaca, NY: Cornell University Press, 2005. Print.
Billington, Michael. "Money and Other Demons: Merchant of Venice." *The Guardian* June 1, 1999. Web.
——. "Theatre Review." *The Guardian* May 14, 2003. Web.
Bloom, Harold. *Shakespeare: The Invention of the Human.* New York: Riverhead, 1998. Print.
Boal, Augusto. *Hamlet and the Baker's Son.* New York: Routledge, 2001. Print.
——. *Legislative Theatre: Using Performance to Make Politics.* New York: Routledge, 1998. Print.
——. *Theatre of the Oppressed.* 1979. New York: Theatre Communications Group, 1993. Print.
Booker, Keith. *Colonial Power, Colonial Texts: India in the Modern British Novel.* Ann Arbor, MI: University of Michigan Press, 1997. Print.
Bourdieu, Pierre. "Forms of Capital." In *Handbook of Theory and Research for the Sociology of Education.* Ed. J. Richardson. New York: Greenwood, 241–258. Print.
Bradley, Laura. *Brecht and Political Theatre: The Mother on Stage.* New York: Oxford University Press, 2006. Print.
Brantley, Ben. "Railing at a Money-Mad World." *New York Times* June 30, 2010. Web.
——. "Review." *New York Times* February 15, 2008. Web.
Brecht, Bertolt. *Brecht on Theatre: The Development of an Aesthetic.* Trans. John Willet. New York: Hill and Wang, 1964. Print.
Coen, Ralph Alan. *ShakesFear and How to Cure It!* Clayton, DE: Prestwick House, 2007. Print.
Davis, Tracy C. and Thomas Postlethwaits, Eds. *Theatricality.* Cambridge: Cambridge University Press, 2004. Print.
Desmet, Christy. "Character Criticism." In *Shakespeare: An Oxford Guide.* Eds. Stanley Wells and Lena Orlin. Oxford: Oxford University Press, 2003. 351–362. Print.
Dolan, Jill. *The Feminist Spectator as Critic.* Ann Arbor, MI: University of Michigan Press, 1988. Print.
Douglas, Amy Scott. *Shakespeare Inside: The Bard Behind Bars.* London: Continuum Press, 2007. Print.

Dunning, Eric G., Patrick J. Murphy, and John Michael Williams. *The Roots of Football Hooliganism: An Historical and Sociological Study*. New York: Routledge and Kegan Paul, 1988. Print.
Elam Jr, Harry J., and David Krasner. *African American Performance and Theater History: A Critical Reader*. Oxford: Oxford University Press, 2001. Print.
Fanconi, Kendra. "Place Remembers." *Canadian Theatre Review* 145 (2011): 97–99. Print.
Fitzpatrick, Lisa. "Staging The Merchant of Venice in Cork: The Concretization of a Shakespeare Play for a New Society." *Modern Drama (MD)* 50.2 (2007): 168–183. Print.
Garber, Marjorie. "Shakespeare as Fetish." In *Shakespeare: The Critical Complex – Post Modern Shakespeare*. Eds. Stephen Orgel and Sean Keilen. New York and London: Garland, 1999. Print.
Gates Jr, Henry Louis. *The Signifying Monkey*. Oxford: Oxford University Press, 1988. Print.
Goodman, Lizbeth. "Women's Alternative Shakespeares and Women's Alternatives to Shakespeare in Contemporary British Theatre." *Cross Cultural Performances: Differences in Women's Revisions of Shakespeare*. Champaign, IL: University of Illinois Press, 1993. Print.
Gray, Leslie. Private Correspondence. September, 2012.
Hartley, Andrew James. *Julius Caesar: Shakespeare in Performance*. Manchester: Manchester University Press, 2013. Print.
———. "Shakespeare and Contemporary Performance Spaces." In *The Edinburgh Companion to Shakespeare and the Arts*. Eds. Mark Thornton Burnett, Adrian Streete, and Ramona Wray. Edinburgh: Edinburgh University Press, 2011. 332–346. Print.
Hartley, L. P. *The Go Between. 1953*. New York: New York Review Books Classics, 2002. Print.
Hubner, Zygmunt. *Theatre & Politics*. Evanston, IL: Northwestern University Press, 1992. Print.
Isherwood, Charles. "Review." *The New York Times* June 23, 2008. Web.
Kelleher, Joe. *Theatre and Politics*. New York: Palgrave Macmillan, 2009. Print.
Kemp, Sandra and Judith Squires. *Feminisms*. Oxford: Oxford University Press, 1997. Print.
Kershaw, Baz. *The Radical in Performance: Between Bracht and Baudrillard*. New York: Routledge, 1999. Print.
Klett, Elizabeth. "Re-Dressing the Balance: All-Female Shakespeare at the Globe Theatre." In *Shakespeare Re-Dressed: Cross Gender Casting in Contemporary Performance*. Ed. James C. Bulman. Madison, NJ: Fairleigh Dickinson University Press, 2008. 166–188. Print.
Knowles, Ric. *Reading the Material Theatre*. Cambridge: Cambridge University Press, 2004. Print.
Loehlin, James. *Henry V: Shakespeare in Performance*. Manchester: Manchester University Press, 2000. Print.
———. "Merchant of Venice Review." *Theatre Journal* 48.1 (1996): 94–96. Print.
Lopez, Jeremy. "Spreading the Shakespeare Gospel: A Rhetorical History of the Academic Theater Review." In *New Directions in Renaissance Drama and Performance Studies*. Ed. Sarah Werner. Basingstoke UK: Palgrave, 2010. 109–130. Print.

Margolies, David. *The Shakespeare Myth*. Ed. Graham Holderness. Manchester: Manchester University Press, 1988. Print.
Mazer, Cary. "My Problem with Shylock." *English Department*. University of Pennsylvania. n.d. Web.
———. "Solanio's Coin." *Shakespeare Bulletin* 21.3 (Fall 2003) 7–46 and 21.4 (Winter 2003): 28–29. Print.
Melnikoff, Kirk. "Review." *Shakespeare Bulletin* 23.3 (2005): 75–80. Print.
Miller, Michael. "Review: TR Warszawa: *Macbeth 2008*." *Berkshire Review* July 9, 2008. Web.
Miola, Robert S. "Julius Caesar and the Tyrannicide Debate." *Shakespeare Quarterly* 38 (1985): 271–289. Print.
"Mission & Vision." *Shakespeare Behind Bars*. n.p., n.d. 2013. Web.
"Our Mission." *Actor's Shakespeare Project*. 2013. Web.
Potter, Lois. *Othello: Shakespeare in Performance*. Manchester: Manchester University Press, 2002. Print.
Rebhorn, Wayne. "The Crisis of the Aristocracy in *Julius Caesar*." *Renaissance Quarterly* 43 (1990): 75–111. Print.
Reeves, Stuart Hampton. *The Henry VI Plays: Shakespeare in Performance*. Manchester: Manchester University Press, 2006. Print.
Richards, David. "Theater Review; Sellar's Merchant of Venice Beach." *The New York Times* October 18, 1994. Web.
Riggio, Milla Cozart. *Teaching Shakespeare Through Performance*. New York: Modern Language Association of America (MLA), 1999. Print.
Rocklin, Edward. *Performance Approaches to Teaching Shakespeare*. Urbana, IL: National Council of Teachers, 2005. Print.
Rossi, Doc. "Brecht on Shakespeare: A Revaluation." *Comparative Drama* 30.2 (1996): 158–187. Print.
Ryzik, Melena. "Scottish Play Gets Polish Makeover." *New York Times* June 11, 2008. Web.
Said, Edward W. *Orientalism*. New York: Random House, 1979. Print.
Salter, Chris. *Entangled: Technology and the Transformation of Performance*. Cambridge, MA: The MIT Press, 2010. Print.
Savran, David. *A Queer Sort of Materializing: Recontextualizing American Theatre*. Ann Arbor, MI: University of Michigan Press, 2003. Print.
Scholz, Sally J. *Feminism: A Beginner's Guide*. Oxford: Oneworld Publications, 2010. Print.
Smallwood, Robert. *Shakespeare Survey* 53 (2000): 269. Print.
Stasio, Marylin. "TR Warszawa's Macbeth 2008." *Variety*. Web.
Taylor, Michael. "The Critical Tradition." In *Shakespeare: An Oxford Guide*. Eds. Stanley Wells and Lena Orlin. Oxford: Oxford University Press, 2003. 323–332. Print.
"The Merchant of Venice." *Corcadorca*. n.p., n.d. Web.
Thomas, Chad Allen. "On Queering Twelfth Night." *Theatre Topics* 20.2 (2011): 101–111. Print.
Thompson, Ayanna. "Blackface Bard: Returning to Shakespeare or Leaving Him." *Shakespeare Bulletin* 27.3 (2009): 437–456. Print.
———. *Colorblind Shakespeare: New Perspectives on Race and Performance*. New York: Routledge, 2006. Print.
———. *Passing Strange: Shakespeare, Race, and Contemporary America*. Oxford: Oxford University Press, 2011. Print.

Tofteland, Curt L. and Hal Cobb. "Prospero Behind Bars." *Shakespeare Survey* 65 (2012): 443. Print.
Tribble, Evelyn B. and John Sutton. "Minds in and Out of Time: Memory, Embodied Skill, Anachronism and Performance." *Textual Practice* 26.4 (2012): 587–607. Print.
Trounstine, Jean. *Shakespeare Behind Bars: The Power of Drama in a Women's Prison.* New York: St. Martin's Press, 2001. Print.
Werner, Sarah. *Shakespeare and Feminist Performance: Ideology on Stage.* New York: Routledge, 2001. Print.
White, John J. *Bertolt Brecht's Dramatic Theory.* Rochester, NY: Camden House, 2004. Print.
Wray, Ramona. "The Morals of *Macbeth* and Peace as Process: Adapting Shakespeare in Northern Ireland's Maximum Security Prison." *Shakespeare Quarterly* 62.3 (2011): 340–643. Print.
Wright, L.S. "Shakespeare in South Africa: Alpha and 'Omega'." *Postcolonial Studies* 7.1 (2004): 18. Print.

Index

Note: Productions are listed by company rather than venue. See also the Annotated Reading List for authors and their works.

Actors' Shakespeare Project (Boston), 105
African American Shakespeare Company, 86–9
Alabama Shakespeare Festival, 82
Aldridge, Ira, 62, 140, 145
Aucoin, Don, 136, 138

Bakhtin, Mikhail, 32
Bardeffect, 103–4, 115, 127
Barnes, Todd Landon, 81, 87–8
Bennet, Benjamin, 3, 29, 32, 55
Billington, Michael, 72–3, 80
Blair, Tony, 80, 98
Bloom, Harold, 46, 61
Boal, Augusto, 5, 24–7, 29, 34, 38, 41, 47, 86–7, 104
   forum theatre, 25–6
   on Shakespeare, 26
   simultaneous dramaturgy, 25
Bogdanov, Michael, 76–80
Booker, M. Keith, 46
Bourdieu, Pierre, 103
Branaugh, Kenneth, 76
Brecht, Bertolt, 4, 12–18, 25, 27, 29, 34, 37–8, 41, 44, 59, 74, 77, 91, 125, 133, 135
   dialectical theatre, 15–16, 34
   epic, 13, 15–16, 34
   on Shakespeare, 16–18
   verfremdungseffekte, 13–15
Brook, Peter, 42, 133, 135
Brustein, Robert, 134–5, 142, 144
Bush, George W., 81, 85, 98–100, 104, 142
Butler, Judith, 36

Callaghan, Dympna, 60
Chekhov, Anton, 16
Churchill, Caryl, 36
Cobb, Hal, 113–14
colour-blind casting, *see* race
Corcadorca, 106–8
Coriolanus, 16–18
cross-gender casting, 66–8
cultural materialism, 39, 41

Daniels, Ron, 95–6
Davis, Tracey C., 15
de Beauvoir, Simone, 35–6
Desmet, Christy, 43
Diamond, Elin, 36
Dillon, John, 3, 98
Dolan, Jill, 37
Douglas, Amy Scott, 111–15, 139
Doran, Greg, 101
Dworkin, Andrea, 36

Edwards, Gale, 60
eugenics, 119

Falklands War, 76, 78–9
Farber, Yael, 100–2
Fascism, 94–5
feminism, 35–7, 40, 43, 53, 121–3
Fiennes, Ralph, 98–9
Fitzpatrick, Lisa, 106–7
Fleetwood, Kate, 82
Foucault, Michel, 36
found space production, 104–6
FOX news, 99–100
Freire, Paulo, 25

Garber, Marjorie, 46
Gates, Henry Louis, 37
George, David, 27
Globe theatre, 44, 66–8, 93
Goodman, Lizbeth, 53–4

Goold, Rupert, 82–5
Gray, Leslie, 125–6

Hall, Edward, 96–7
Hall, Peter, 42
Hamlet, 26
Hampton-Reeves, Stuart, 158 n.5
Hands, Terry, 95
hate groups, 121
Henry V, 76–81
Hicks, Greg, 96
Historical contextualization and the theatre, 44–5
 see also new historicism
Hitler, Adolf ,91
Hodgdon, Barbara, 43, 60
Holderness, Graham, 46
Hopkins, Anthony, 62
Hubner, Zygmunt, 5, 18–21, 27
 on propaganda, 20
 on Shakespeare, 21
Hunter, Kathryn, 66
Hussein, Saddam, 80
Hytner, Nicholas, 80

Ibsen, Henrich, 16
identity politics, 35–43

Jarzyna, Grzegorz, 83–4
Jim Crow, 119
Jones, James Earl, 62
Julius Caesar, 90–102
 Georgia Shakespeare, 1–3, 98, 102

Kelleher, Joe, 15
Kershaw, Baz, 5, 27–30, 32, 140, 146
 radical performance, 28
King, Rodney, 69
Klett, Elizabeth, 158 n.5
Knowles, Ric, 5, 21–4, 26–7, 32, 34, 47–8, 79–80
 On Shakespeare, 23–4
Kott, Jan, 21, 42

Lester, Adrian, 80
literary criticism, 37
Loehlin, James, 69–71, 77
Long, Huey, 98
Lopez, Jeremy, 103

Macbeth, 39–40, 43, 81–8, 111, 132–3, 142
Macbush, 81, 85
Mandela, Nelson, 91–2
Margolies, David, 46
Marrowitz, Charles, 65
Mazer, Cary, 61–2
McDiamid, Ian, 77
McTeer, Janet, 66
Melnikoff, Kirk, 112–13
The Merchant of Venice, 59, 61–2, 63, 69–73, 106–8, 113
Meyerhold, Vsevelod, 12
Mickey B, 111
A Midsummer Night's Dream, 117–28
Miller, Jonathan, 62
Miss Saigon, 28, 30
Morrison, Conall, 82

National Endowment for the Arts, 81–2, 85, 104
new criticism, 43
new historicism, 39, 41
Noble, Adrian, 76
Nunn, Trevor, 65, 72–3

Obama, Barack, 116–17
Olivier, Laurence, 62, 75–6
Only Animal, 105–6
Oregon Shakespeare Festival, 136–7
Othello, 59, 60, 62–6

Papp, Joseph, 133–4
Patrick Henry College, 131–3, 141–2
Pennington, Michael, 77–8
Pimlott, Steven, 95
Piscator, Erwin, 4, 12–13, 16
Potter, Lois, 64
Punch Drunk, 105

Quarshie, Hugh, 60
Queer theory, *see* sexual orientation

Race, 37, 39, 54, 101, 119–21, 125–6, 139–40, 142–3
 cross and "colour blind" casting, 52–3, 60–1, 62–6, 68–9, 101, 119–21, 142–3
Realism, 16

Rich, Adrienne, 36
Richard II, 21
Richards, David, 70–1
Richter, Falk, 99–100
Robeson, Paul, 62
Romeo and Juliet, 145–6
Rossi, Doc, 18

Said, Edward, 37
Savran, David, 38
Scholz, Sally J., 36
Sellars, Peter, 69–71, 72, 133
September 11th 2001 terrorist attacks, 3, 80, 98
sexual orientation, 37–8, 54–5, 125–6
Schechner, Richard, 27
Shakespeare
  audience demographics, 49, 136–8, 144–5
  authorship question, 47
  characters, 41–3
  education, 46, 50, 108–11, 146–7
  and the "establishment", 48–53
  in prison, 111–15
  and the Victorians, 46, 53
  see also individual play titles
Shakespeare Behind Bars, 111–15, 139
Shakespeare in Action, 117
Shaw, Fiona, 54
Simpson, O.J., 62
Sleep No More, 105
social media, 138

soccer hooliganism, 77–9
Stanislavski, Constantine, 2, 12, 14
Stewart, Patrick, 63–6, 82–5

Tea Party, 116, 141
Thacker, David, 96
Thatcher, Margaret, 76, 78–9, 95
The Taming of the Shrew, 59–60, 66–9, 121
theatrical semiotics, 1–3, 11–12, 22, 32, 43–4, 50–1, 53
Thomas, Chad Allen, 55
Thompson, Ayanna, 44, 54, 60–1, 131–48
Tofteland, Curt T., 112–15
Toneelgroep, 100
Troustine, Jean, 111–15
TR Warszawa, 83–5, 87
Twelfth Night, 50

University of North Carolina, Charlotte, 116–27

Vance, Carol, 36

Warner, Deborah, 98–9
Welles, Orson, 94, 135
Werner, Sarah, 43–4, 59–60
Williams, Raymond, 28
Wilson, August, 134, 142
Worthen, W.B., 21, 142
Wray, Ramona, 159 n.9